Inviting friends over for nibblies and a drink is good fun all round. A finger-food occasion allows you to indulge your creative urges in the planning and preparation of the food, and cater for far more people at one time – without the restrictions inherent in a three-course dinner party. To help you on your way, *New Finger Food* contains a veritable treasure trove of ideas for making both hot and cold hors d'oeuvres, sensible party-planning advice, do-ahead cooking tips and suggestions for serving – the only thing left for you to do is get busy on that invitation list. Enjoy!

Pamela Clark

Food Director

contents

planning a party

Great finger food – fantastic to look at and easy to prepare – is perhaps the most important component of a successful party. And it's also the most fun – planning the menu and preparing the individual dishes is both creative and satisfying. This book not only provides you with recipes that will have your guests screaming "encore!", it also features handy hints on how to host, prepare and plan a party for any occasion.

get organised

Being organised saves you money and prevents you from becoming stressed. Accomplish all you can in the lead-up to your party; make a list of what can be done each day of the week before the event. Most of our recipes tell you how far in advance they can be made, and this will help you plan your time. With a little forethought, you will find yourself happily mingling with your friends on the night, confident that everything's going to plan.

the guests

Who's coming must figure in your party-planning equation. Very different menus are required for a welcome to the new boss or a welcome-home for one of the gang. Once you know who your guests are, deciding what to serve them becomes a whole lot easier. You might have to include some dishes for those who are watching their weight or are vegetarian; consider also whether any guests have food allergies or observe dietary restrictions due to their religion.

know your limitations

It's a good idea to serve a mixture of cold and hot savouries. Most of the recipes in this book come with one hot and one cold accompanying finger food suggestion to help you make your selection. But know your limitations: it is better to choose a few dishes that go well together than to be over-ambitious and make too many.

choice of food

Choose your selection of finger food and drinks taking into consideration the nature of the occasion, the season, time of day, duration of the event and the number of people. Hosting drinks for eight friends before going out for dinner makes very different demands on you than does a full-blown open-house that stretches over the better part of a Sunday. A casual gathering out on the patio in summer requires a different menu and bar list than does a formal mid-winter affair. When choosing the recipes, think about complementary colours, textures and flavours. The time of year determines what people like to eat – and what produce is available – so the month you choose will also act as a guide to the kind of menu you should create. Serve light dishes in the summer and more robust bites in winter. Remember to check on the food requirements of your guests beforehand – vegetarian, kosher, low fat, etc.

invitations

It's best to give your guests at least two weeks notice for your party, whether this is done by mail, e-mail or telephone. Be sure to inform your guests exactly what type of party you will be holding so that they can dress accordingly. Be as clear as possible as to the exact location of your party, and it's also handy to give guests added information such as parking and/or transport facilities. Don't forget to include an RSVP date; this will help you decide on the quantity of food and drink you need to provide.

how much food?

Making sure you provide the right amount of food is paramount to the success of your party. Below is some advice to help you decide how much food you should make.

• For pre-dinner nibbles: allow 4 to 5 pieces of food per person.

• For a cocktail party: allow 4 to 5 pieces of food per person for the first hour and then 4 pieces of food for each hour after that.

• For the full afternoon or evening: allow 12 to 14 pieces of food per person for the duration of the whole party.

drinks

Drinks quantities can often be harder to estimate than food. There is a general rule that 10 guests will consume 20 drinks on average at a cocktail party. If it's a full-evening affair, this increases to 40 drinks. One budget-conscious tip is to offer a selection of cocktails made from one or two primary spirits only, or just limit the choice to wine and beer. Regardless of the time of year of your party, the one thing you can never have too much of is ice. There is nothing worse than serving warm drinks. If you have limited space in your fridge and freezer, a good idea is to store the ice and drinks in the dishwasher. Place the cans and bottles in the racks and cover them with ice; you can chill your glasses in here too. The drinks are out of harm's way, are insulated and will remain cold, and the melted ice drains out below – too easy!

A laundry tub or a kiddies' wading pool are other good places to keep your drinks chilled in ice. Make sure you have a bag or two of "clean" ice on hand too, so people can add it to their cocktails if they wish.

hiring help

If you plan to have 20 or more guests, consider getting extra help. This help could be a waiter or two, chefs or a bar person. If hiring professional help, get a number of quotes from different companies – this may save you money. You could also contact hospitality schools to see if any of their students would like to get some practical training.

If you are restricted in your budget and hiring extra help is out of the question, consider recruiting family members or friends. It's important to give all helpers specific responsibilities. Once you have the help organised, spend a little time briefing them about how many guests there will be, when you will be serving certain foods, the layout of the venue and the location of all the kitchen supplies and equipment.

Below is a rough guide to show you how many varieties of food and drink are needed for a 2-hour cocktail party for varying numbers of guests.

NO. OF GUESTS	8	15	25	35	50
dips	2 varieties	2 varieties	2 varieties	3 varieties	3 varieties
cold finger food	2 varieties	3 varieties	3 varieties	4 varieties	5 varieties
hot finger food	2 varieties	3 varieties	3 varieties	4 varieties	5 varieties
wine (incl. sparkling)	4 bottles	7 bottles	12 bottles	17 bottles	25 bottles
cocktails	2 varieties	2 varieties	3 varieties	3 varieties	4 varieties
soft drinks (incl. juice, water, etc.) 2-litre	4 varieties	4 varieties	4 varieties	4 varieties	4 varieties

checklist

Here is a brief checklist to help you prepare for your party. If you don't own enough cutlery or a certain type of equipment, borrow from a friend or phone a party hire company. There are plenty of the latter about, and their charges are reasonable.

- forks and spoons
- airtight storage containers
- plates
- fridge and freezer space
- serving trays and platters
- small tables
- oven trays
- tea and coffee equipment
- napkins
- decorations
- glasses or plastic cups
- music
- bowls for dips
- garbage bins
- hot plates
- coasters
- chairs
- marquee (if outdoors)
- fans or heaters

shortcuts

Here are a few suggestions if you're pressed for time.

- Remember that you can prepare some food a few weeks in advance and freeze it.
- There is an immense amount of prepared food at your local supermarket. Different types of bottled antipasto or a cheese platter can be put together in minutes. Dips can be purchased from your local supermarket – all you have to do is present them in attractive serving bowls.
- Crackers and chips make excellent dippers for your dips.
- Cold meats and seafood can easily be arranged on a large platter, and look fantastic with little effort.
- Use bottled ingredients, such as pesto or tapenade, instead of making your own.
- Buy prepared sushi from your local Japanese takeaway, but make sure you do this at the last minute – sushi must be absolutely fresh.

COCKTAILS

cosmopolitan

PREPARATION TIME 5 MINUTES

Combine 1 cup ice cubes, 10ml lemon vodka, 20ml vodka, 30ml Cointreau, 60ml cranberry juice and 10ml fresh lime juice in a cocktail shaker. Shake vigorously; strain into a chilled 150ml cocktail glass. Garnish with a twist of lime rind.

makes 1

sugar syrup

Sugar syrup will keep for about 2 months in refrigerator.
Combine 1 cup (220g) caster sugar and 1 cup (250ml) water in small saucepan; stir over low heat until sugar dissolves. Bring to a boil, reduce heat; simmer, uncovered, without stirring, 5 minutes. Remove from heat; cool. Makes about 1½ cups (375ml)

caipiróska

PREPARATION TIME 5 MINUTES

Cut 1 lime into eight wedges. Using mortar and pestle, crush 1 tablespoon palm sugar with six of the lime wedges. Combine lime mixture with 1/2 cup ice cubes, 60ml vodka and 10ml sugar syrup in a cocktail shaker. Shake vigorously; pour over 1/2 cup crushed ice in a chilled 180ml sugar-rimmed old-fashioned glass. Garnish with remaining lime wedges.

makes 1

margarita

PREPARATION TIME 5 MINUTES

You can use triple sec or white curaçao instead
of Cointreau, if you prefer.

Combine 1 cup ice cubes, 45ml tequila, 30ml fresh
lime juice and 30ml Cointreau in a cocktail shaker.
Shake vigorously; strain into a salt-rimmed chilled
150ml margarita glass. Garnish with lime wedges.

makes 1

long island iced tea

PREPARATION TIME 5 MINUTES

Place 1 cup ice cubes in a 300ml highball glass; add
30ml vodka, 30ml tequila, 30ml white rum, 30ml gin,
15ml Cointreau, 15ml lemon juice, 15ml sugar syrup
and 30ml cola. Stir with swizzle stick. Garnish with a
twist of lemon rind and fresh mint sprig.

makes 1

chocolate martini

PREPARATION TIME 5 MINUTES

Trace outline of 12cm-circle with chocolate
Ice Magic onto a flat plate. Working quickly, twist
the rim of a 150ml cocktail glass in Ice Magic; sit
glass upright in freezer to set. Combine 1/2 cup ice
cubes, 45ml vodka and 45ml crème de cacao in a
cocktail shaker. Shake vigorously; strain into glass.
Combine another 1/2 cup ice cubes, 20ml Baileys
and 10ml framboise liqueur in same shaker. Shake
vigorously; pour carefully over back of a spoon into
glass so mixture floats. Do not stir. Garnish with small
chocolate curls and a fresh raspberry.

makes 1

fallen angel

PREPARATION TIME 5 MINUTES

The classic Fallen Angel is made with crème de menthe,
but our version calls for gin and blue curaçao, which
gives the cocktail an amazing colour.

Combine 45ml gin, 30ml blue curaçao, 25ml fresh
lemon juice and a dash of Angostura Bitters in a
chilled 350ml piña colada glass. Add 1 cup ice
cubes; top with 60ml lemonade. Garnish with
a maraschino cherry.

makes 1

mango daiquiri

PREPARATION TIME 5 MINUTES

Peel half of a medium-sized ripe mango; chop flesh coarsely. Blend or process mango with 1 cup ice cubes, 30ml white rum, 30ml mango liqueur and 15ml fresh lime juice until just combined. Pour into a chilled 180ml tulip-shaped glass. Garnish with a fresh cherry.

makes 1

mudslide

PREPARATION TIME 5 MINUTES

Drizzle the inside of a 400ml fountain glass with chocolate Ice Magic; freeze until chocolate sets and glass is chilled. Blend or process 15ml vodka, 15ml Baileys, 15ml Kahlua, 15ml thickened cream, 1 scoop vanilla ice-cream, 1 scoop chocolate ice-cream and 1/2 cup crushed ice until just combined. Pour mixture into prepared glass. Garnish with chocolate curls.

makes 1

tuna salad on pitta crisps

Blend or process 180g can tuna with 1 tablespoon each of yogurt, mayonnaise and prepared horseradish; stir in finely chopped green onion and parsley to taste. Serve on toasted pitta triangles.

herbed-ricotta spread with rye dippers

Combine 400g ricotta with 1/2 cup finely grated parmesan cheese and finely chopped black olives, chives and fresh thyme. Serve cold with toasted rye bread fingers.

ricotta and fetta dip

Process 200g each of fetta and ricotta with 1/2 cup sour cream, 2 tablespoons each of lemon juice and olive oil, and 1 clove garlic until smooth. Serve cold with a platter of crudités.

tapenade

Process 375g seeded kalamata olives, 2 cloves garlic, 5 anchovies, and 2 tablespoons each of capers and lemon juice. Add 1/3 cup olive oil; process until smooth. Serve with grissini.

cucumber croûtes

Process 250g cream cheese with 1 large avocado; add lemon juice and sambal oelek to taste. Pipe or spoon onto slices of cucumber; top each with canned flaked red salmon and green onion slices.

liptauer

Process 60g softened butter and 250g cream cheese with 1 small onion, 3 anchovies, 8 cornichons, and paprika, capers and caraway seeds to taste. Serve with pumpernickel squares.

parmesan walnut wafers

Combine 1 cup finely grated parmesan cheese and 2 tablespoons finely chopped walnuts; drop rounded teaspoons of mixture on baking-paper-lined oven tray, sprinkle with fresh thyme. Brown in hot oven; stand until set.

sun-dried tomato aïoli and prawn canapés

Combine 1 cup mayonnaise with 2 tablespoons sun-dried tomato pesto and 2 cloves crushed garlic; spread onto toasted baguette slices, top each with 1 prawn and 1 fresh basil leaf.

vietnamese rice paper rolls
PREPARATION TIME 50 MINUTES **COOKING TIME** 15 MINUTES

DO AHEAD Chicken can be cooked and dipping sauce made a day ahead. Cover separately; refrigerate until required.

1 tablespoon peanut oil
2 chicken breast fillets (340g)
24 x 17cm-square rice paper sheets
1 small red capsicum (150g), sliced thinly
1¼ cups (100g) bean sprouts
1 cup firmly packed fresh mint leaves
1 cup firmly packed fresh coriander leaves
DIPPING SAUCE
1 clove garlic, crushed
2 tablespoons fish sauce
¼ cup (60ml) lime juice
¼ cup (60ml) oyster sauce
¼ cup (65g) finely grated palm sugar
2 red thai chillies, seeded, chopped finely

1 Heat oil in small frying pan; cook chicken until browned all over and cooked through. Stand 10 minutes; slice thinly into 24 pieces.
2 Place one sheet of rice paper in medium bowl of warm water until just softened; carefully lift from water. Place on board; pat dry with absorbent paper. Position rice paper in diamond shape; place chicken slice vertically down centre of rice paper, top with capsicum, sprouts, mint and coriander. Fold bottom corner over filling; roll rice paper from side to side to enclose filling. Repeat with remaining rice paper sheets and filling.
3 Serve rice paper rolls cold with dipping sauce.
DIPPING SAUCE Combine ingredients in small saucepan; stir over medium heat until sugar dissolves. Refrigerate until cold.

makes 24
per roll 1.7g fat; 317kJ (76 cal)
per tablespoon dipping sauce 0.1g fat; 128kJ (30 cal)

goes well with
peking duck wraps (page 16)
gyoza with soy vinegar sauce (page 86)

peking duck wraps

PREPARATION TIME 25 MINUTES

DO AHEAD Buy a whole large barbecued duck from a Chinese food shop the day before serving this recipe. Remove and discard skin and bones; slice the meat thinly. Cover; refrigerate until required.

8 green onions, trimmed
1/4 cup (60ml) hoisin sauce
1 tablespoon plum sauce
2 cups (250g) thinly sliced
  barbecued duck meat
16 small butter lettuce leaves

1 Cut white section of onion from green section. Dip green sections in medium bowl of boiling water for 5 seconds, then place in medium bowl of cold water; drain. Thinly slice white sections.

2 Divide combined sauces, duck and slices of white section of onion among lettuce leaves. Roll lettuce to enclose filling; tie each wrap with one piece of green section of onion to secure.

3 Serve peking duck wraps cold or at room temperature.

makes 16
per wrap 4.3g fat; 560kJ (62 cal)

TIP You may need extra green onions to ensure you have enough green sections to wrap the lettuce leaves.

goes well with
pork satay (page 93)
oysters osaka (page 21)

smoked trout on crispy wonton wrappers

PREPARATION TIME 30 MINUTES   **COOKING TIME** 10 MINUTES

DO AHEAD Buy a 400g whole smoked trout for this recipe. The day before serving, remove and discard skin and bones; shred the meat coarsely. Cover; refrigerate until required.

1 tablespoon prepared
   horseradish
1 tablespoon lemon juice
½ cup (120g) sour cream
2 tablespoons finely chopped
   fresh chives
1½ cups (260g) smoked trout
12 wonton wrappers
vegetable oil, for deep-frying
50g snow pea tendrils
1 tablespoon coarsely chopped
   fresh chives, extra

1 Combine horseradish, juice, sour cream and chives in small bowl; fold in trout.
2 Cut each wrapper into four squares. Heat oil in wok or large saucepan; deep-fry wrappers, in batches, until crisp. Drain on absorbent paper.
3 Divide snow pea tendrils among wrappers; top each with 1 heaped teaspoon of the trout mixture, sprinkle with extra chives.
4 Serve immediately.

makes 48
per wrapper 1.5g fat;
100kJ (24 cal)

goes well with
salmon tartare (page 22)
tikka prawns with raita (page 60)

radicchio with thai crab salad

PREPARATION TIME 20 MINUTES (PLUS REFRIGERATION TIME) **COOKING TIME** 5 MINUTES

DO AHEAD Dressing can be made a day ahead. Cover; refrigerate until required. Crab salad can be assembled up to 4 hours ahead. Cover; refrigerate until required.

¼ cup (60ml) water
¼ cup (60ml) lime juice
2 tablespoons sugar
2 red thai chillies, seeded, chopped finely
500g fresh crab meat
1 lebanese cucumber (130g), seeded, chopped finely
1 small red capsicum (150g), chopped finely
2 green onions, sliced thinly
6 radicchio

1 Combine the water, juice, sugar and chilli in small saucepan; stir over heat, without boiling, until sugar dissolves. Bring to a boil; remove from heat, cool. Cover; refrigerate dressing until cold.
2 Combine crab, cucumber, capsicum, onion and dressing in medium bowl.
3 Trim ends from radicchio; separate leaves (you need 64 leaves). Place 1 heaped teaspoon of the crab salad on each leaf.
4 Serve cold.

makes 64
per leaf 0.1g fat; 38kJ (9 cal)

TIP We used radicchio, but you can also use red or green witlof, if you prefer.

goes well with
thai coconut prawns (page 61)
mussels with chilli-lime sauce (page 25)

prawn remoulade

PREPARATION TIME 25 MINUTES

DO AHEAD Remoulade can be made up to a day ahead. Cover; refrigerate until required.

3 egg yolks
1 tablespoon white
 wine vinegar
1 tablespoon wholegrain
 mustard
1/4 cup (60ml) water
1 1/3 cups (330ml) vegetable oil
2 tablespoons drained capers,
 chopped finely
2 tablespoons fresh dill,
 chopped coarsely
48 medium cooked
 prawns (1.2kg)

1 Blend or process yolks, vinegar, mustard and the water until smooth. With motor operating, gradually add oil in a thin, steady stream; process until mixture thickens. Transfer mixture to medium serving bowl; stir in capers and dill. Cover; refrigerate remoulade until cold.
2 Shell and devein prawns, leaving tails intact. Arrange prawns on serving platter.
3 Serve cold with remoulade.

makes 2 cups remoulade
per prawn 0.1g fat; 44kJ (11 cal)
per tablespoon remoulade
13.4g fat; 505kJ (121 cal)

goes well with
rumaki (page 107)
crab dip (page 44)

oysters osaka

PREPARATION TIME 20 MINUTES

DO AHEAD Dressing can be made up to 2 days ahead. Cover; refrigerate until required.

⅓ cup (80ml) mirin
2 tablespoons rice vinegar
2 teaspoons lemon juice
½ teaspoon wasabi paste
2 red thai chillies, seeded, chopped finely
32 oysters, on the half shell
sea salt, for serving

1   Combine mirin, vinegar, juice, wasabi and chilli in small jug.
2   Remove oysters from shells; reserve shells. Drain oysters on absorbent paper; wash and dry shells. Return oysters to shells; sit on a bed of sea salt on serving platter. Divide dressing over oysters.
3   Serve cold.

makes 32
per oyster 0.3g fat; 44kJ (11 cal)

goes well with
bruschetta niçoise (page 28)
mini prawn cocktails (page 32)

salmon tartare

PREPARATION TIME 30 MINUTES

DO AHEAD Tartare ingredients can be chopped up to 3 hours ahead of combining. Cover separately; refrigerate until required.

2 tablespoons lemon juice
2 teaspoons prepared horseradish
1 tablespoon drained capers, chopped finely
2 tablespoons finely chopped fresh chives
250g sashimi salmon, chopped finely
1 small red onion (100g), chopped finely
1 packet (80g) mini toasts
1/4 cup (65g) crème fraîche
40 small fresh dill sprigs

1   Combine juice, horseradish, capers and chives in medium bowl; add salmon and onion, toss gently to combine.
2   Divide salmon tartare among mini toasts; top each with crème fraîche and a dill sprig.
3   Serve cold.

makes 40
per toast 0.9g fat; 107kJ (25 cal)

TIP Salmon sold as sashimi salmon has met stringent guidelines regarding its treatment since leaving the water, so you can be guaranteed of its quality and that it's safe to eat raw.

goes well with
bloody mary oyster shots (page 24)
grilled swordfish and snow pea skewers (page 67)

bloody mary oyster shots

PREPARATION TIME 10 MINUTES

DO AHEAD Bloody mary mixture can be made a day ahead. Cover; refrigerate until required.

You need 16 shot glasses for this recipe.

16 oysters
2 tablespoons vodka
2 tablespoons lemon juice
3/4 cup (180ml) tomato juice
1/4 teaspoon Tabasco sauce
1 teaspoon worcestershire sauce

1 Place one oyster in each glass.
2 Combine remaining ingredients in medium jug; divide mixture among glasses.
3 Serve cold.

makes 16
per shot 0.3g fat; 44kJ (16 cal)

goes well with
california handrolls (page 50)
quesadilla wedges (page 57)

mussels with chilli-lime sauce

PREPARATION TIME 10 MINUTES

DO AHEAD Chilli-lime sauce can be made a day ahead. Cover; refrigerate until required.

32 cooked mussels,
   on the half shell
¼ cup (60ml) sweet
   chilli sauce
1 tablespoon tequila
⅓ cup (80ml) lime juice
1 tablespoon finely chopped
   fresh coriander

1 Loosen mussels in shell.
2 Combine remaining ingredients in medium jug; divide mixture among mussels.
3 Serve cold.

makes 32
per mussel 0.2g fat;
52kJ (13 cal)

goes well with
lime and soy wings (page 81)
smoked salmon cones (page 35)

thai chicken salad in crispy wonton cups

PREPARATION TIME 40 MINUTES **COOKING TIME** 15 MINUTES

2 chicken breast fillets (340g)
40 wonton wrappers
cooking-oil spray
1/4 small chinese cabbage (100g), shredded finely
1 small carrot (70g), grated finely
3 green onions, sliced thinly
2 tablespoons sesame seeds, toasted
DRESSING
1/3 cup (80ml) peanut oil
1 tablespoon white vinegar
1 tablespoon brown sugar
1 tablespoon light soy sauce
1 teaspoon sesame oil
1 clove garlic, crushed

DO AHEAD Wonton cups can be made up to 2 days ahead. Keep in an airtight container. Chicken mixture can be prepared and refrigerated, covered, up to 3 hours ahead.

You need four 12-hole mini (1 1/2 tablespoons/30ml) muffin pans for this recipe. If you do not own that many, make the wonton cups in batches, placing the cooked ones on a wire rack while you bake the remainder.

1 Poach chicken, covered in boiling water, in small frying pan. Reduce heat; simmer, uncovered, about 10 minutes or until cooked through. Drain chicken; stand 10 minutes, chop finely.
2 Preheat oven to moderately hot. Lightly oil four 12-hole mini muffin pans.
3 Using 7.5cm-round cutter, cut one round from each wonton wrapper. Push rounds carefully into holes of prepared pans; spray lightly with oil.
4 Bake, uncovered, in moderately hot oven about 7 minutes or until wonton cups are golden brown. Stand in pans 2 minutes; turn onto wire racks to cool.
5 Meanwhile, combine chicken in large bowl with cabbage, carrot, onion, sesame seeds and dressing.
6 Divide chicken salad among wonton cups, pressing down gently to fill.
7 Serve immediately.
   DRESSING Combine ingredients in screw-topped jar; shake well.

makes 40
per cup 2.8g fat; 186kJ (44 cal)

goes well with
gyoza with soy vinegar sauce (page 86)
rösti with smoked trout and crème fraîche (page 46)

BRUSCHETTA

We suggest using either wood-fired Italian bread or French baguettes for the bruschetta. Bruschetta slices can be toasted a day ahead. Keep at room temperature in an airtight container.

onion marmalade and semi-dried tomato bruschetta

PREPARATION TIME 25 MINUTES
COOKING TIME 10 MINUTES

⅓ cup (80ml) olive oil
3 cloves garlic, crushed
2 x 30cm bread sticks
vegetable oil, for shallow-frying
48 fresh sage leaves
1 cup (340g) onion marmalade
¾ cup (110g) semi-dried tomatoes

1 Combine olive oil and garlic in small bowl. Trim ends from bread sticks; cut sticks into 1cm slices. Brush both sides of bread pieces with garlic oil; toast under hot grill until bruschetta are browned lightly both sides.
2 Heat vegetable oil in medium saucepan; quickly shallow-fry sage, in batches, until just crisp (do not allow to burn). Drain on absorbent paper.
3 Divide marmalade among bruschetta; top with one tomato and a sage leaf.
4 Serve at room temperature.

makes 48
per bruschetta 2.2g fat; 187kJ (45 cal)

bruschetta niçoise

PREPARATION TIME 35 MINUTES
COOKING TIME 10 MINUTES

⅓ cup (80ml) olive oil
3 cloves garlic, crushed
2 x 30cm bread sticks
1 tablespoon drained baby capers
1 medium egg tomato (75g), seeded, chopped finely
1 trimmed stick celery (75g), chopped finely
¼ cup (30g) seeded black olives, chopped finely
180g can tuna in olive oil, drained, flaked
5 drained anchovy fillets, chopped finely
1 small red onion (100g), chopped finely
2 tablespoons lemon juice

1 Combine oil and garlic in small bowl. Trim ends from bread sticks; cut sticks into 1cm slices. Brush both sides of bread pieces with garlic oil; toast under hot grill until bruschetta are browned lightly both sides.
2 Combine capers, tomato, celery, olives, tuna, anchovy, onion and juice in medium bowl. Divide niçoise mixture among bruschetta.
3 Serve at room temperature.

makes 48
per bruschetta 2.2g fat; 171kJ (41 cal)

haloumi and tapenade bruschetta

PREPARATION TIME 30 MINUTES
COOKING TIME 15 MINUTES

1/3 cup (80ml) olive oil
3 cloves garlic, crushed
2 x 30cm bread sticks
250g haloumi
1/3 cup (60g) tapenade
48 baby basil leaves

1 Combine oil and garlic in small bowl. Trim ends from bread sticks; cut sticks into 1cm slices. Brush both sides of bread pieces with garlic oil; toast under hot grill until bruschetta are browned lightly both sides.
2 Cut cheese into 48 squares. Heat large lightly oiled non-stick frying pan; cook cheese, in batches, until browned lightly both sides.
3 Divide tapenade among bruschetta; top with cheese and a basil leaf.
4 Serve at room temperature.

makes 48
per bruschetta 2.7g fat; 190kJ (45 cal)

artichoke and roasted capsicum bruschetta

PREPARATION TIME 30 MINUTES
COOKING TIME 25 MINUTES

1 small yellow capsicum (150g)
1/3 cup (80ml) olive oil
3 cloves garlic, crushed
2 x 30cm bread sticks
1/4 cup (65g) basil pesto
250g marinated artichoke hearts,
   drained, sliced thinly
48 fresh flat-leaf parsley leaves

1 Quarter capsicum; discard seeds and membranes. Roast under grill or in very hot oven, skin-side up, until skin blisters and blackens; cover capsicum with paper or plastic for 5 minutes. Peel away skin; slice thinly.
2 Combine oil and garlic in small bowl. Trim ends from bread sticks; cut sticks into 1cm slices. Brush both sides of bread pieces with garlic oil; toast both sides.
3 Divide pesto, artichoke and capsicum among bruschetta; top with a parsley leaf.
4 Serve at room temperature.

makes 48
per bruschetta 2.9g fat; 193kJ (46 cal)

Originally from Russia, blini are small, leavened buckwheat pancakes that are traditionally served with sour cream and caviar. They make a perfect base for any number of canapé toppings.

buckwheat blini

PREPARATION TIME 10 MINUTES
COOKING TIME 20 MINUTES

DO AHEAD Blini can be made up to 2 days ahead. Cover; refrigerate until required. Bring to room temperature before adding topping.

1/2 cup (75g) buckwheat flour
1/4 cup (35g) plain flour
1 1/2 teaspoons baking powder
1 egg, beaten lightly
3/4 cup (180ml) buttermilk
30g butter, melted

1 Sift flours and baking powder into medium bowl, gradually whisk in combined egg and buttermilk; stir in butter.
2 Cook blini, in batches, by dropping 2-teaspoon portions of batter into large heated non-stick frying pan; turn blini, cook until browned on other side. Turn blini onto wire racks to cool.

makes 48

crème fraîche with salmon roe

PREPARATION TIME 10 MINUTES

1/4 cup (65g) crème fraîche
1 tablespoon coarsely chopped fresh chives
50g salmon roe

1 Divide crème fraîche, chives and roe among 16 blini.
2 Serve at room temperature.

makes 16
per blin 1.8g fat; 122kJ (29 cal)

smoked chicken and mustard

PREPARATION TIME 10 MINUTES

¼ cup (75g) whole egg mayonnaise
1 tablespoon mild english mustard
200g boneless smoked chicken, sliced thinly
32 small fresh oregano leaves

1 Combine mayonnaise and mustard in small bowl.
2 Divide chicken and mayonnaise mixture among 16 blini; top with oregano.
3 Serve at room temperature.

makes 16
per blin 5.1g fat; 290kJ (69 cal)

smoked salmon and dill

PREPARATION TIME 10 MINUTES

¼ cup (60g) sour cream
1 teaspoon finely chopped fresh dill
1 tablespoon finely chopped red onion
1 teaspoon finely grated lemon rind
¼ teaspoon freshly ground black pepper
1 tablespoon drained capers, chopped finely
100g smoked salmon slices, chopped coarsely
16 small fresh dill sprigs

1 Combine sour cream, dill, onion, rind, pepper and capers in small bowl.
2 Divide sour cream mixture and salmon among 16 blini; top with dill.
3 Serve at room temperature.

makes 16
per blin 2.5g fat; 167kJ (40 cal)

mini prawn cocktails

PREPARATION TIME 30 MINUTES

DO AHEAD Cocktail sauce can be made up to 2 days ahead.
Cover; refrigerate until required.

32 medium cooked prawns (800g)
1/3 cup (100g) whole egg mayonnaise
2 tablespoons cream
1 tablespoon tomato sauce
1 teaspoon worcestershire sauce
1/2 teaspoon Tabasco sauce
1 teaspoon prepared horseradish
2 baby cos lettuces
1 tablespoon coarsely chopped fresh chives
1 tablespoon finely grated lemon rind

1 Shell and devein prawns.
2 Whisk mayonnaise, cream, sauces and horseradish in small bowl.
3 Trim ends from lettuces; separate leaves (you need 32 leaves).
   Top each leaf with one prawn; divide cocktail sauce over prawns
   then sprinkle with chives and rind.
4 Serve immediately.

makes 32
per cocktail 3g fat; 180kJ (43 cal)

goes well with
smoky eggplant caviar (page 45)
filet mignons with béarnaise sauce (page 104)

bocconcini, olive and cherry tomato skewers with pesto

PREPARATION TIME 25 MINUTES

DO AHEAD Pesto can be made up to 2 days ahead. Cover; refrigerate until required.

You need 32 long cocktail toothpicks for this recipe.

½ cup (40g) finely grated
   parmesan cheese
½ cup (80g) toasted pine nuts
2 cloves garlic, crushed
1 cup (250ml) extra virgin
   olive oil
2 cups firmly packed fresh
   basil leaves
16 cherry tomatoes, halved
32 baby bocconcini (450g)
32 medium seeded
   green olives (110g)

1 Blend or process cheese, nuts, garlic and half of the oil until combined. Add basil and remaining oil; process until almost smooth. Transfer pesto to serving bowl.
2 Thread one tomato half, one bocconcini and one olive onto each toothpick.
3 Serve cold with pesto.

makes 32
per skewer 2.2g fat;
142kJ (34 cal)
per tablespoon pesto
14.1g fat; 549kJ (131 cal)

goes well with
mini reubens (page 63)
mini zucchini frittatas (page 38)

smoked salmon cones

PREPARATION TIME 40 MINUTES (PLUS REFRIGERATION TIME)

DO AHEAD Cheese mixture can be made up to a day ahead. Cover; refrigerate until required.

800g smoked salmon slices
300ml cream
125g packet cream
   cheese, softened
1/4 cup (50g) toasted pistachios,
   chopped finely
2 tablespoons finely chopped
   fresh chives
48 baby spinach leaves (100g)

1 Blend or process 100g of the salmon until chopped finely. Add cream and cheese; process until smooth. Transfer mixture to medium bowl; stir in nuts and chives. Refrigerate until firm.
2 Halve remaining salmon slices widthways; place one spinach leaf on each salmon slice, top with 1 teaspoon of the cheese mixture. Roll each into small cone to enclose filling.
3 Place cones on serving tray, cover; refrigerate 2 hours.
4 Serve cold.

makes 48
per cone 4.5g fat;
247kJ (59 cal)

goes well with
crab dip (page 44)
greek mini pizzas (page 115)

35

profiteroles with salmon mousse

PREPARATION TIME 35 MINUTES **COOKING TIME** 30 MINUTES

DO AHEAD Unfilled profiteroles can be baked up to 2 days ahead.
Keep at room temperature in an airtight container.

80g butter, chopped
1 cup (250ml) water
1 cup (150g) plain flour
4 eggs, beaten lightly
200g smoked salmon slices
SALMON MOUSSE
250g tub spreadable cream cheese
1/2 cup (125ml) cream
1 tablespoon lemon juice
1/4 teaspoon Tabasco sauce
210g can red salmon, drained
1 tablespoon drained capers
1/2 small red onion (50g), chopped finely
1 tablespoon finely chopped fresh dill

1 Preheat oven to hot. Lightly oil oven trays.
2 Combine butter and the water in small saucepan; bring to a boil.
   Add sifted flour; beat with wooden spoon over heat until mixture
   comes away from base and side of saucepan to form a smooth ball.
3 Transfer mixture to small bowl; beat in eggs, one at a time,
   with electric mixer until mixture becomes glossy.
4 Spoon mixture into piping bag fitted with 1cm plain tube; pipe
   small mounds of choux pastry 5cm apart onto prepared trays
   (you will have 60 unbaked profiteroles).
5 Bake, uncovered, in hot oven 10 minutes. Reduce oven to moderate;
   bake further 10 minutes or until profiteroles are browned lightly and crisp.
   Turn profiteroles onto wire racks to cool.
6 Halve profiteroles; scoop out any soft centres. Divide salmon mousse
   equally among profiterole bases; top each with one slice of the salmon
   then cover with top half of profiterole.
7 Serve at room temperature.
   SALMON MOUSSE Blend or process cheese, cream, juice, sauce,
   salmon and capers until smooth; stir in onion and dill.

makes 60
per profiterole 4.2g fat; 236kJ (56 cal)

goes well with
crème fraîche with salmon roe blini (page 30)
goat cheese and roasted capsicum mini melts (page 62)

mini zucchini frittatas

PREPARATION TIME 20 MINUTES **COOKING TIME** 15 MINUTES

DO AHEAD Frittata mixture can be prepared up to 2 hours ahead but not baked until just before serving. Cover; refrigerate until required.

You need four 12-hole non-stick mini (1½ tablespoons/30ml) muffin pans for this recipe. If you do not own that many, make the frittatas in batches, placing the cooked ones on a wire rack while you bake the remainder.

8 eggs
1 cup (240g) sour cream
¼ cup finely chopped
   fresh chives
1 large yellow zucchini (150g),
   grated coarsely
1 large green zucchini (150g),
   grated coarsely
⅓ cup (25g) finely grated
   parmesan cheese
2 tablespoons coarsely
   chopped fresh chives, extra

1 Preheat oven to moderate. Lightly oil four 12-hole mini muffin pans.
2 Whisk eggs with two-thirds of the sour cream in large bowl until smooth; stir in chives, zucchini and cheese.
3 Divide mixture among holes of prepared pans. Bake, uncovered, in moderate oven 15 minutes; turn onto wire rack to cool. Top frittatas with remaining sour cream and extra chives.
4 Serve at room temperature.

makes 48
per frittata 3.1g fat;
142kJ (34 cal)

goes well with
cottage pies (page 84)
prawn remoulade (page 20)

cheese balls with four coatings

PREPARATION TIME 40 MINUTES (PLUS REFRIGERATION TIME)

DO AHEAD Za'atar and pepper coatings can be prepared a day ahead. Store at room temperature in an airtight container.

500g neufchâtel cheese
500g farm cheese
2 teaspoons finely grated
   lemon rind
2 tablespoons lemon juice
1/4 teaspoon sea salt

1 Line four oven trays with baking paper.
2 Blend or process ingredients until smooth; refrigerate about 2 hours or until firm enough to roll.
3 Using hands, roll rounded teaspoons of the mixture into balls; place 16 balls on each of prepared trays. Refrigerate, covered, until firm.
4 Roll 16 balls in each of the four coatings.
5 Serve cold.

makes 64

pepper coating

Coat balls in a mixture of 1 1/2 tablespoons poppy seeds and 2 teaspoons cracked black pepper.

per ball 4.5g fat; 217kJ (52 cal)

parsley coating

Coat balls in 1/4 cup finely chopped fresh flat-leaf parsley.

per ball 4.4g fat; 210kJ (50 cal)

sesame seed coating

Coat balls in 1/4 cup (35g) sesame seeds.

per ball 4.7g fat; 224kJ (53 cal)

za'atar coating

Combine 1 tablespoon each of sumac and toasted sesame seeds, 1 teaspoon each of dried oregano, dried marjoram and sweet paprika, and 2 teaspoons dried thyme; coat balls in mix.

per ball 4.5g fat; 217kJ (52 cal)

TIP Za'atar, a Middle-Eastern spice blend, can be purchased from Middle-Eastern specialty stores.

goes well with
laila's lamb kofta with spiced yogurt (page 58)
smoky eggplant caviar (page 45)

turkish spinach dip

PREPARATION TIME 10 MINUTES (PLUS REFRIGERATION AND COOLING TIME) **COOKING TIME** 10 MINUTES

DO AHEAD Dip can be made a day ahead. Cover; refrigerate until required.

You need 1 bunch of spinach weighing 300g for this recipe.

1 tablespoon olive oil
1 small brown onion (80g),
  chopped finely
1 clove garlic, crushed
1 teaspoon ground cumin
1/2 teaspoon curry powder
1/4 teaspoon ground turmeric
100g trimmed spinach leaves,
  shredded finely
500g thick yogurt

1 Heat oil in medium frying pan; cook onion and garlic, stirring, until onion softens. Add spices; cook, stirring, until fragrant. Add spinach; cook, stirring, until spinach wilts. Transfer mixture to serving bowl; cool.
2 Stir yogurt through mixture, cover; refrigerate 1 hour.
3 Serve cold with toasted pitta.

makes 2 cups
per tablespoon 2.3g fat;
144kJ (34 cal)

goes well with
haloumi and tapenade
bruschetta (page 29)
laila's lamb kofta with
spiced yogurt (page 58)

blue cheese and caramelised onion dip

PREPARATION TIME 20 MINUTES   **COOKING TIME** 15 MINUTES

DO AHEAD Dip can be made a day ahead. Cover; refrigerate until required.

1 tablespoon olive oil
1 medium brown onion (150g), chopped finely
1 medium pear (230g), chopped coarsely
½ cup (150g) mayonnaise
½ cup (125ml) cream
150g danish blue cheese

1 Heat oil in medium frying pan; cook onion, stirring constantly, about 10 minutes or until onion is browned and slightly caramelised. Add pear; cook 5 minutes. Cool.

2 Blend or process mayonnaise, cream and cheese until smooth; transfer to serving bowl. Stir in onion mixture.

3 Serve at room temperature with toasted rye bread fingers.

makes 2 cups
per tablespoon 7.1g fat; 337kJ (81 cal)

goes well with
pancetta and gruyère potato bites (page 83)
pecan chicken salad finger sandwiches (page 54)

ocean trout sashimi rolls with lemon dipping sauce

PREPARATION TIME 25 MINUTES (PLUS STANDING TIME) **COOKING TIME** 5 MINUTES

DO AHEAD Lemon dipping sauce can be made a day ahead.
Cover; refrigerate until required.

Ocean trout sold as sashimi ocean trout has met stringent guidelines
regarding its treatment since leaving the water, so you can be guaranteed
of its quality and that it's safe to eat raw.

200g sashimi ocean trout
1/4 medium red capsicum (50g)
1/2 lebanese cucumber (65g)
1 green onion, trimmed
LEMON DIPPING SAUCE
1/2 cup (125ml) rice vinegar
1/4 cup (55g) caster sugar
2 teaspoons light soy sauce
1/2 teaspoon finely grated lemon rind

1   Using sharp knife, cut trout into paper-thin slices (you need 16 slices).
2   Remove and discard seeds and membranes from capsicum; halve
    cucumber lengthways, scoop out seeds. Halve onion lengthways.
    Slice capsicum, cucumber and onion into 8cm-long pieces.
3   Lay trout slices on board in single layer; divide capsicum, cucumber and
    onion among trout slices, mounding at one of the narrow edges. Roll
    slices around filling; place rolls, seam-side down, on serving platter.
4   Serve immediately with lemon dipping sauce.
    LEMON DIPPING SAUCE Heat vinegar, sugar and sauce in small
    saucepan, stirring, until sugar dissolves. Remove from heat, add rind;
    stand 10 minutes. Strain sauce into serving bowl; discard rind.

makes16
per roll 0.5g fat; 64kJ (15 cal)
per tablespoon sauce 0g fat; 121kJ (29 cal)

goes well with
tuna and cucumber mini maki (page 49)
fish cakes with mirin dipping sauce (page 108)

crab dip

PREPARATION TIME 15 MINUTES

DO AHEAD Dip can be made up to 4 hours ahead. Cover; refrigerate until required.

200g packaged cream cheese
¼ cup (75g) mayonnaise
2 tablespoons lime juice
1 tablespoon sweet chilli sauce
1 dill pickle (50g),
    chopped finely
2 x 170g cans crab meat,
    drained, flaked
2 tablespoons finely chopped
    fresh coriander

1 Beat cheese, mayonnaise, juice and sauce in small bowl with electric mixer until smooth. Transfer to serving bowl; fold in remaining ingredients.
2 Serve cold with toasted french bread slices.

makes 2 cups
per tablespoon 3.8g fat;
196kJ (47 cal)

goes well with
mussel kebabs with
walnut sauce (page 90)
smoked trout on crispy
wonton wrappers (page 17)

smoky eggplant caviar

PREPARATION TIME 15 MINUTES (PLUS COOLING TIME) **COOKING TIME** 30 MINUTES

DO AHEAD Caviar can be made a day ahead. Cover; refrigerate until required.

2 large eggplants (1kg)
⅓ cup (80ml) lemon juice
¼ cup (60ml) olive oil
1 clove garlic, crushed

1 Pierce eggplants all over with skewer or sharp knife. Cook on heated oiled grill plate (or grill or barbecue) about 30 minutes or until eggplant softens, turning every 10 minutes. Cool.
2 Halve eggplants, scoop flesh out of skin into fine strainer; discard skin. Drain 5 minutes.
3 Blend or process eggplant until pulpy; transfer to serving bowl. Stir in remaining ingredients.
4 Serve cold or at room temperature with grissini.

makes 2 cups
per tablespoon 2.4g fat;
113kJ (27 cal)

goes well with
cheese balls with four
coatings (page 39)
grilled lamb cutlets with
tomato compote (page 91)

rösti with smoked trout and crème fraîche

PREPARATION TIME 30 MINUTES (PLUS COOLING TIME) **COOKING TIME** 25 MINUTES

DO AHEAD Buy a 400g whole smoked trout for this recipe.
The day before serving, remove and discard skin and bones;
shred the meat coarsely. Cover; refrigerate until required.

1kg potatoes
2 tablespoons coarsely chopped fresh chives
15g butter, melted
1/2 cup (125ml) olive oil
1 1/2 cups (260g) smoked trout, flaked
1/3 cup (85g) crème fraîche
1 tablespoon coarsely chopped fresh chives, extra

1 Boil, steam or microwave unpeeled whole potatoes for 5 minutes;
  drain. Cool potatoes for 20 minutes, peel away skin; grate coarsely.
  Combine potato in medium bowl with chives and butter.
2 Heat half of the oil in medium frying pan. Shape level tablespoons of the
  potato mixture into patties; cook half of the patties until browned and crisp
  both sides. Drain on absorbent paper. Repeat with remaining oil and patties.
3 Divide trout and crème fraîche among rösti; top with extra chives.
4 Serve immediately.

makes 32
per rösti 4.9g fat; 292kJ (70 cal)

goes well with
turkish spinach dip (page 40)
chive pancakes with sausages and caramelised onion (page 102)

sushi rice

PREPARATION TIME
10 MINUTES (PLUS DRAINING AND STANDING TIME)
COOKING TIME
12 MINUTES (PLUS STANDING TIME)

DO AHEAD Sushi rice can be made up to 4 hours ahead. Cover; refrigerate until required.

1 cup (200g) koshihikari rice
1 cup (250ml) water
SUSHI VINEGAR
2 tablespoons rice vinegar
1 tablespoon sugar
¼ teaspoon salt

1 Place rice in large bowl, fill with cold water, stir with one hand; drain. Repeat process two or three times until water is almost clear. Drain rice in strainer 30 minutes.
2 Meanwhile, prepare sushi vinegar.
3 Place drained rice and the water in medium saucepan, cover tightly; bring to a boil. Reduce heat; simmer, covered tightly, on low heat about 12 minutes or until water is absorbed. Remove from heat; allow rice to stand, covered, 10 minutes.
4 Spread rice in a large non-metallic bowl. Using large flat wooden spoon or plastic spatula, repeatedly slice through rice at a sharp angle to break up lumps and separate grains, gradually pouring in sushi vinegar. Not all of the vinegar may be required; the rice shouldn't become wet.
5 Continue to lift and turn rice with spoon, from outside to centre of bowl, for about 5 minutes or until rice is almost cool. Cover rice with damp cloth while making sushi variations of your choice.

SUSHI VINEGAR Stir combined vinegar, sugar and salt in small bowl until sugar dissolves.

makes 2 cups

tuna and cucumber mini maki

PREPARATION TIME 30 MINUTES

4 sheets toasted
    seaweed (yaki-nori)
1 portion sushi rice (see left)
2 teaspoons wasabi paste
120g piece sashimi tuna,
    cut into 5mm strips
1 lebanese cucumber (130g),
    seeded, cut into thin strips
¼ cup (60ml) japanese
    soy sauce

1 Fold one sheet of seaweed in
   half parallel with lines marked on
   rough side of sheet; cut along
   fold. Place a half sheet, shiny-
   side down, lengthways across
   bamboo mat about 2cm from
   edge closest to you.
2 Dip fingers in bowl of vinegared
   water; shake off excess. Mould
   ¼ cup of the rice into oblong
   shape; place across centre
   half of seaweed.
3 Wet fingers again; gently rake
   rice evenly over seaweed,
   leaving 2cm strip at far end
   of seaweed uncovered.
4 Using finger, swipe a dab of
   wasabi across centre of rice,
   flattening it out evenly.
5 Place tuna strips, end to end, in
   a row over wasabi across centre
   of rice; repeat with cucumber.
6 Starting with edge closest to
   you, pick up mat with thumb and
   index finger of both hands; use
   remaining fingers to hold filling
   in place as you roll mat. Roll
   forward, pressing gently but
   tightly, wrapping seaweed
   around rice and filling. When
   roll is complete, the strip of
   uncovered seaweed will stick
   to the roll to form a join.
7 Unroll mat; place sushi roll,
   join-down, on board. Wipe very
   sharp knife with damp cloth; cut
   roll into six pieces of mini maki.
8 Working quickly, repeat process
   with remaining seaweed, rice,
   wasabi, tuna and cucumber.

9 Serve mini maki immediately, at
   room temperature, with soy sauce
   and more wasabi, if desired.

makes 48
per mini maki 0.2g fat;
89kJ (21 cal)

CHICKEN TERIYAKI VARIATION
You can make another easy
mini maki by replacing the tuna
and cucumber with 2 chicken
tenderloins (150g) that have

been marinated for 1 hour in
2 tablespoons teriyaki sauce,
then cooked through and sliced
thinly. Follow the method above
to step 5, substituting slices
of teriyaki chicken and 2 thinly
sliced green onions for the
tuna and cucumber; continue
with rolling from step 6.

makes 48
per mini maki 0.2g fat;
94kJ (22 cal)

california handrolls

PREPARATION TIME 45 MINUTES

10 sheets toasted
   seaweed (yaki-nori)
1/3 cup (100g) mayonnaise
1 teaspoon wasabi paste
1 portion sushi rice (page 48)
60g cooked crab, shredded
1 lebanese cucumber (130g),
   seeded, sliced thinly
1 small avocado (200g),
   sliced thinly
1 small red capsicum (150g),
   sliced thinly

1 Cut each sheet of seaweed into
   4 squares. Combine mayonnaise
   and wasabi in small bowl.
2 Place a quarter sheet of
   seaweed, shiny-side down,
   diagonally across palm of left
   hand. Dip fingers of right hand in
   bowl of vinegared water; shake
   off excess. Mould rounded
   teaspoons of rice into oblong
   shape; place across centre of
   seaweed. Wet fingers; gently
   rake rice evenly over seaweed,
   making a slight groove down the
   middle of the rice for filling. Using
   finger, swipe a dab of wasabi
   mayonnaise along the groove,
   top with a little crab, cucumber,
   avocado and capsicum.
3 Fold one side of seaweed over;
   fold other side of seaweed over
   the first to form a cone. Tip of
   cone can be folded back to
   hold cone shape securely.
4 Serve at room temperature.

makes 40
per handroll 1.6g fat;
155kJ (37 cal)

SMOKED SALMON VARIATION Substitute 100g finely sliced smoked
salmon, 2 teaspoons finely grated lemon rind and 3 finely shredded
green onions for the crab, cucumber and avocado. In step 1, add
1 teaspoon lemon juice to the wasabi and mayonnaise mixture.
Continue to step 2, filling the groove with a little of the smoked
salmon, rind and onion; continue with rolling from step 3.

makes 40
per handroll 1.1g fat; 137kJ (33 cal)

sydney ura-maki

PREPARATION TIME 20 MINUTES

2 sheets toasted seaweed
(yaki-nori), halved lengthways
4 cups prepared sushi
rice (page 48)
2 teaspoons red pepper mix
(shichimi togarashi)
2 teaspoons black
sesame seeds
2 teaspoons white
sesame seeds
1½ tablespoons wasabi paste
1 small avocado (200g),
sliced thinly
200g sashimi salmon,
cut into 1cm strips
¼ cup (60ml) japanese
soy sauce

1 Place one half-sheet of seaweed lengthways across bamboo mat about 2cm from the edge of mat closest to you. Dip fingers of one hand in bowl of vinegared water, shake off excess; pick up a quarter of the rice, press onto seaweed then, working from left to right, gently rake rice to cover seaweed completely and evenly.

2 Sprinkle quarter of the pepper mix and quarter of the combined sesame seeds over rice then cover rice completely with plastic wrap. Carefully lift mat, turn over so seaweed faces up; place back on bamboo mat about 2cm from edge. Using finger, swipe a dab of wasabi across centre of seaweed then top with about a quarter of the avocado and salmon, making certain the filling extends to ends of seaweed.

3 Starting with edge closest to you, pick up mat with thumb and index finger of both hands; use remaining fingers to hold filling in place as you roll mat. Roll forward, pressing gently but tightly, wrapping rice around filling. Continue rolling forward to complete the roll. Unroll mat; keep roll in plastic wrap.

4 Wipe sharp knife with damp cloth; cut roll, still in plastic wrap, in half then each half into quarters, wiping knife between each cut. Remove plastic wrap.

5 Serve ura-maki at room temperature with remaining wasabi and sauce.

makes 32
per ura-maki 1.8g fat;
297kJ (71 cal)

TIP To prevent them from drying out, keep finished ura-maki wrapped in plastic, uncut, until ready to serve.

goes well with

chicken yakitori with sesame dipping sauce (page 92)
oysters osaka (page 21)

BLT on mini toasts

PREPARATION TIME 20 MINUTES
COOKING TIME 5 MINUTES

4 bacon rashers (280g)
1 packet (80g) mini toasts
6 butter lettuce leaves
¼ cup (75g) whole egg mayonnaise
200g grape tomatoes, halved

1 Remove rind from bacon; cut each rasher into
   pieces slightly smaller than mini toasts. Heat large
   frying pan; cook bacon, stirring, until browned
   and crisp, drain on absorbent paper.
2 Cut lettuce into pieces slightly larger than mini toasts.
3 Divide mayonnaise among mini toasts; top each
   with lettuce, bacon and tomato.
4 Serve at room temperature.

makes 40
per BLT 2.1g fat; 136kJ (33 cal)

turkey, brie and cranberry on pumpernickel rounds

PREPARATION TIME 30 MINUTES

300g brie
120g thinly sliced smoked turkey breast
24 packaged cocktail pumpernickel rounds
¼ cup (80g) whole-berry cranberry sauce
1 tablespoon coarsely chopped fresh chives

1 Cut cheese into small, thin slices.
2 Divide cheese and turkey equally among
   pumpernickel rounds; top each with
   cranberry sauce and chives.
3 Serve at room temperature.

makes 24
per round 4g fat; 318kJ (76 cal)

tandoori chicken on naan

PREPARATION TIME
30 MINUTES (PLUS MARINATING TIME)
COOKING TIME 15 MINUTES

500g chicken breast fillets
1/4 cup (80g) tandoori paste
200g yogurt
2 tablespoons coarsely chopped fresh mint
1 tablespoon lemon juice
4 pieces naan (500g)
32 small fresh mint leaves

1 Combine chicken, paste and 1/4 cup of the yogurt
in medium bowl; toss to coat chicken all over.
Cover; refrigerate 3 hours or overnight.
2 Cook chicken on heated oiled grill plate (or grill or
barbecue) until browned and cooked through; stand
10 minutes. Slice chicken; cut into small pieces.
3 Combine remaining yogurt, mint and juice in small
bowl. Cut 32 x 4cm rounds from naan. Spread
about 1/2 teaspoon of the yogurt mixture on each
round; top with chicken, another 1/2 teaspoon of
the yogurt mixture and mint leaf.
4 Serve cold.

makes 32
per naan 3.4g fat; 355kJ (85 cal)

roast beef with caramelised onion on rye

PREPARATION TIME 20 MINUTES
COOKING TIME 30 MINUTES

500g beef fillet
1 tablespoon olive oil
2 large red onions (600g), sliced thinly
1 tablespoon brown sugar
1 tablespoon red wine vinegar
1 loaf rye bread (660g)
1/4 cup (60ml) olive oil, extra
2 tablespoons mild english mustard
40 fresh flat-leaf parsley sprigs

1 Preheat oven to moderate. Cook beef in medium
heated oiled frying pan until browned all over; place in
small baking dish. Roast, uncovered, in moderate oven
20 minutes or until cooked as desired. Wrap beef in foil.
2 Meanwhile, heat oil in same pan; cook onion until soft.
Add sugar and vinegar; cook, stirring, until caramelised.
3 Discard ends from bread. Cut bread into 1.5cm slices;
cut each slice into quarters. Brush bread both sides
with extra oil; toast both sides.
4 Slice beef thinly. Spread mustard on bread; top with
parsley, beef and onion. Serve at room temperature.

makes 40
per piece 2.8g fat; 325kJ (78 cal)

FINGER SANDWICHES

You can use any sliced bread variety, cut into the shape you prefer, for these finger sandwiches.

creamy egg and lettuce

PREPARATION TIME 30 MINUTES

DO AHEAD Egg filling can be made a day ahead. Cover; refrigerate until required.

18 hard-boiled eggs, chopped finely
1/2 cup (150g) whole egg mayonnaise
2 tablespoons cream
1/4 cup finely chopped fresh chives
48 slices wholemeal bread
1 small iceberg lettuce, trimmed,
   shredded finely
80g butter, softened

1 Combine egg, mayonnaise, cream and chives in large bowl. Divide half of the egg mixture among 16 slices of the bread; divide half of the lettuce among the egg-topped slices.
2 Butter 16 slices of the remaining bread both sides; place each slice on top of lettuce. Divide remaining egg mixture among sandwiches; top with remaining lettuce and remaining bread slices.
3 Remove crusts; cut sandwiches into thirds.
4 Serve at room temperature.

   makes 48
   per finger sandwich 5.5g fat; 474kJ (113 cal)

pecan chicken salad

PREPARATION TIME 40 MINUTES

DO AHEAD Chicken filling can be made a day ahead. Cover; refrigerate until required.

Buy a 1kg cooked chicken for this recipe.

3 cups (480g) finely chopped cooked chicken
4 green onions, chopped finely
1/2 cup (50g) pecans, chopped finely
3 trimmed sticks celery (225g), chopped finely
1/2 cup (150g) whole egg mayonnaise
1/3 cup (80g) sour cream
20 slices white bread
10 slices brown bread

1 Combine chicken, onion, nuts, celery, mayonnaise and sour cream in large bowl.
2 Spoon 2 tablespoons of the chicken mixture onto each of 10 slices of white bread; top each with a slice of brown bread. Top each with another 2 tablespoons of chicken mixture; top with remaining white bread.
3 Remove crusts; cut sandwiches into triangles.
4 Serve at room temperature.

   makes 40
   per finger sandwich 5.6g fat; 409kJ (98 cal)

red salmon and green onion

PREPARATION TIME 20 MINUTES

DO AHEAD Sandwiches can be made up to
1 hour ahead. Cover; refrigerate until required.

2 x 415g cans red salmon, drained
½ cup (150g) whole egg mayonnaise
12 green onions, chopped finely
20 slices white bread

1 Discard any skin or bones from salmon. Combine
  salmon with mayonnaise and onion in medium bowl.
2 Divide salmon mixture among 10 slices of the bread;
  top with remaining bread slices.
3 Remove crusts; cut sandwiches into quarters.
4 Serve at room temperature.

makes 40
per finger sandwich 5.1g fat; 369kJ (88 cal)

ham and gruyère

PREPARATION TIME 15 MINUTES

DO AHEAD Sandwiches can be made up to
1 hour ahead. Cover; refrigerate until required.

⅓ cup (95g) wholegrain mustard
32 slices brown bread
250g gruyère cheese, sliced thinly
360g thinly sliced leg ham
6 large dill pickles (300g), sliced thinly

1 Divide mustard among 16 slices of the bread. Divide
  cheese, ham and pickle among mustard-topped
  bread slices; top with remaining bread slices.
2 Remove crusts; cut sandwiches into thirds.
3 Serve at room temperature.

makes 48
per finger sandwich 2.1g fat; 250kJ (60 cal)

tostada triangles

Blend or process 425g canned Mexican-style beans; heat beans with ½ cup bottled salsa. Add ⅓ cup sour cream; spread on flour tortilla triangles, top with grated cheddar cheese. Bake in hot oven until cheese melts; top with fresh coriander leaves.

bacon and corn puffs

Mix 250g chopped bacon pieces, 3 finely chopped green onions, 125g can creamed corn and ⅓ cup grated cheddar cheese; spoon onto toasted bread rounds spread with english mustard. Bake in hot oven until cheese melts.

mini ham and pineapple jaffles

Combine 150g shaved leg ham, ½ cup drained crushed pineapple and ½ cup grated cheddar cheese. Divide among buttered bread slices, buttered-side out; cook in preheated sandwich press (or jaffle-maker). Cut into quarters to serve.

prosciutto and cheese-wrapped asparagus

Cut prosciutto slices in half; top with a small piece of fontina cheese. Wrap cheese and prosciutto slices around asparagus spears. Grill until prosciutto is crisp.

quesadilla wedges

Sandwich baby spinach leaves, sliced salami, char-grilled capsicum and grated mozzarella cheese between large burrito tortillas; brush tortillas with oil. Cook on grill plate (or grill or barbecue) until heated through; cut into wedges.

pizza chips

Top large whole corn chips with a little pizza sauce, thin slices of cabanossi or salami and small pieces of cheddar cheese; place on oven tray under preheated grill until cheese melts.

barbecued duck and ginger tartlets

Divide 2 cups shredded barbecued duck meat among 32 x 4cm tartlet cases. Combine $1/4$ cup hoisin sauce and 2 teaspoons grated fresh ginger; divide mixture among tartlets. Heat in hot oven; top with green onion slices.

pigs in blankets

Cut 2 sheets ready-rolled puff pastry into 16 squares each; wrap a cocktail frankfurt in each square, brush with lightly beaten egg. Bake in hot oven, on baking-paper-lined oven tray, until pastry is golden brown. Serve with tomato sauce and mild mustard.

laila's lamb kofta with spiced yogurt

PREPARATION TIME 30 MINUTES (PLUS REFRIGERATION TIME) **COOKING TIME** 20 MINUTES

DO AHEAD Uncooked kofta and spiced yogurt can be made a day ahead. Cover separately; refrigerate until required.

¼ cup (40g) burghul
500g minced lamb
1 egg
1 medium brown onion (150g), chopped finely
¼ cup (40g) pine nuts, chopped finely
2 tablespoons finely chopped fresh mint
2 tablespoons finely chopped fresh flat-leaf parsley
vegetable oil, for shallow-frying
SPICED YOGURT
2 red thai chillies, seeded, chopped finely
1 tablespoon finely chopped fresh mint
1 tablespoon finely chopped fresh flat-leaf parsley
1 tablespoon finely chopped fresh coriander
1 clove garlic, crushed
½ teaspoon ground cumin
500g thick yogurt

1 Cover burghul with cold water in small bowl; stand 10 minutes. Drain; pat dry with absorbent paper to remove as much water as possible.
2 Using one hand, combine burghul in large bowl with lamb, egg, onion, nuts and herbs. Roll rounded teaspoons of the lamb mixture into kofta balls. Place on tray, cover; refrigerate 30 minutes.
3 Heat oil in large frying pan; shallow-fry kofta, in batches, until browned all over and cooked through. Drain on absorbent paper.
4 Serve hot with spiced yogurt.
SPICED YOGURT Combine ingredients in medium bowl.

makes 40
per kofta 3.8g fat; 205kJ (49 cal)
per tablespoon spiced yogurt 1.5g fat; 109kJ (26 cal)

goes well with
cheese balls with four coatings (page 39)
spicy lamb and pine nut triangles (page 99)

tikka prawns with raita

PREPARATION TIME 20 MINUTES **COOKING TIME** 10 MINUTES

DO AHEAD Uncooked prawns can be marinated and raita made a day ahead. Cover separately; refrigerate until required.

24 large uncooked king
   prawns (1.2kg)
1/4 cup (70g) tikka paste
1 1/2 cups (420g) yogurt
1/4 cup finely chopped
   fresh coriander
1/2 teaspoon ground cumin

1 Shell and devein prawns, leaving tails intact.
2 Combine paste and 1/2 cup of the yogurt in small bowl.
3 Cook prawns, in batches, on heated oiled grill plate (or grill or barbecue), brushing prawns with paste mixture, until just changed in colour.
4 Meanwhile, combine remaining yogurt in small bowl with coriander and cumin.
5 Serve prawns hot, with raita.

makes 24
per prawn 0.8g fat;
132kJ (32 cal)
per tablespoon raita
0.6g fat; 54kJ (13 cal)

goes well with
curry puffs with
chutney dip (page 72)
tandoori chicken
on naan (page 53)

thai coconut prawns

PREPARATION TIME 30 MINUTES **COOKING TIME** 15 MINUTES

DO AHEAD Prawns can be skewered and dipping sauce made a day ahead. Cover; refrigerate until required.

You need 24 bamboo skewers; soak them in cold water for at least an hour prior to use.

24 medium uncooked
   prawns (600g)
1/4 cup (35g) plain flour
2 eggs, beaten lightly
1 1/2 cups (100g)
   shredded coconut
1/2 cup (125ml) sweet chilli sauce
2 tablespoons water
2 tablespoons coarsely
   chopped fresh coriander

1 Preheat oven to moderate. Lightly oil two oven trays.
2 Shell and devein prawns. Coat prawns in flour, shake away excess; dip into egg, then coat in coconut.
3 Thread one prawn on each skewer; place, in single layer, on prepared trays. Bake, uncovered, in moderate oven about 15 minutes or until prawns are cooked through.
4 Meanwhile, combine remaining ingredients in small bowl.
5 Serve hot with dipping sauce.

makes 24
per prawn 3.2g fat;
202kJ (48 cal)
per tablespoon sauce
0.4g fat; 61kJ (15 cal)

goes well with
vietnamese rice paper
rolls (page 14)
fish cakes with mirin dipping
sauce (page 108)

goat cheese and roasted capsicum mini melts

PREPARATION TIME 20 MINUTES **COOKING TIME** 25 MINUTES

DO AHEAD Capsicum can be roasted up to 3 days ahead. Cover; refrigerate until required.

2 large red capsicums (700g)
¼ cup (60ml) olive oil
1 clove garlic, crushed
1 long loaf pide
200g firm goat cheese,
   sliced thinly
48 baby basil leaves

1   Quarter capsicums; discard
    seeds and membranes. Roast
    under grill or in very hot oven,
    skin-side up, until skin blisters and
    blackens; cover capsicum with
    plastic or paper for 5 minutes.
    Peel away skin; slice thinly.
2   Meanwhile, combine oil and
    garlic in small bowl. Halve bread
    lengthways; slice into 1.5cm
    pieces, brush one cut-side only
    with garlic mixture. Toast bread,
    oiled-side only, under hot grill
    until browned lightly.
3   Divide cheese among toasted
    sides of bread pieces; top with
    capsicum slices. Grill until heated
    through; top with basil leaves.
4   Serve hot.

makes 48
per melt 2.1g fat; 193kJ (46 cal)

goes well with
cheese scones (page 101)
smoked chicken and
mustard blini (page 31)

mini reubens

PREPARATION TIME 20 MINUTES
COOKING TIME 5 MINUTES

DO AHEAD Corned beef and cheese can be cut a few hours ahead. Cover separately; refrigerate until required.

8 slices rye bread
2 tablespoons thousand
   island dressing
1/2 cup (80g) sauerkraut, drained
100g corned beef, sliced thinly
8 slices packaged swiss cheese

1 Using 4.5cm-round cutter, cut four rounds from each bread slice; place on oven trays. Toast rounds under hot grill until browned lightly both sides.
2 Spread dressing evenly over one side of each round; top each with sauerkraut and beef. Cut each cheese slice into four squares; place on top of beef. Grill until cheese melts.
3 Serve hot.

makes 32
per reuben 2.4g fat;
202kJ (48 cal)

goes well with
cheeseburgers (page 64)
mini prawn cocktails (page 32)

cheeseburgers

PREPARATION TIME 20 MINUTES (PLUS REFRIGERATION TIME) **COOKING TIME** 20 MINUTES

DO AHEAD Uncooked burger patties can be prepared
a day ahead. Cover; refrigerate until required.

200g beef mince
2 green onions, chopped finely
2 tablespoons barbecue sauce
3/4 cup (75g) packaged breadcrumbs
1 egg
1 clove garlic, crushed
6 hamburger buns
2 tablespoons tomato sauce
1 tablespoon american mustard
4 slices packaged cheddar cheese
1 large dill pickle (50g), sliced thinly

1 Using one hand, combine beef, onion, barbecue sauce, breadcrumbs,
   egg and garlic in medium bowl. Using hands, shape beef mixture into
   24 patties. Place on tray, cover; refrigerate 10 minutes.
2 Heat large lightly oiled non-stick frying pan; cook patties, in batches, until
   browned both sides and cooked as desired. Cover patties to keep hot.
3 Meanwhile, slice buns in half horizontally. Using 4cm-round cutter,
   cut four rounds from each bun half; place on oven trays. Toast buns,
   cut-side up, under hot grill until browned lightly.
4 Combine tomato sauce and mustard in small bowl; divide mixture
   evenly among bun bases. Cut each slice of cheese into six rectangles.
   Top each bun base with pickle slice, hot patty, cheese then bun top.
5 Serve hot.

makes 24
per burger 2.7g fat; 381kJ (91 cal)

TIP If burgers start to cool, reheat them in a moderate oven.
If burger buns are not sitting level on top, flatten them with
a board or rolling pin.

goes well with
deep-fried onion rings (page 95)
BLT on mini toasts (page 52)

grilled salmon on lemon grass skewers

PREPARATION TIME 30 MINUTES **COOKING TIME** 20 MINUTES

DO AHEAD Uncooked fish can be skewered and sour cream sauce made up to 4 hours ahead. Cover separately; refrigerate until required.

10 x 30cm lemon grass stems
2kg salmon fillets
2/3 cup (160g) sour cream
1 tablespoon coarsely
   chopped fresh dill
1 tablespoon lemon juice

1 Trim lemon grass tops; cut off hard base of stem. Cut remaining sticks in half lengthways then widthways; you will have 40 lemon grass skewers.
2 Remove any skin or bones from fish; cut fish into 40 x 3cm pieces. Using tip of small knife, cut slit through centre of each piece of fish; thread each piece on a lemon grass skewer. Cook, in batches, on heated oiled grill plate (or grill or barbecue) until salmon is browned lightly all over and cooked as desired.
3 Meanwhile, combine remaining ingredients in small bowl.
4 Serve hot with sour cream sauce.

makes 40
per skewer 3.6g fat;
297kJ (71 cal)
per tablespoon sauce
6.4g fat; 253kJ (60 cal)

goes well with
sydney ura-maki (page 51)
tarragon and lime scallops
(page 70)

grilled swordfish and snow pea skewers

PREPARATION TIME 20 MINUTES **COOKING TIME** 10 MINUTES

DO AHEAD Uncooked fish and snow peas can be skewered up to 4 hours ahead. Cover; refrigerate until required.

You need 24 bamboo skewers; soak them in cold water for at least an hour prior to use, to prevent splintering or scorching.

400g swordfish steak
24 large snow peas (120g)
2 teaspoons Tabasco sauce
1/4 cup (60ml) lemon juice
2 tablespoons olive oil

1 Remove skin and bones from fish; cut fish into 24 long thin slices. Thread each slice, with one snow pea, on a skewer; brush with half of the combined remaining ingredients.
2 Cook skewers, in batches, on heated oiled grill plate (or grill or barbecue), brushing constantly with remaining Tabasco mixture, until fish is browned lightly and cooked as desired.
3 Serve hot.

makes 24
per skewer 1.9g fat;
139kJ (33 cal)

goes well with
oysters with pesto butter
(page 87)
mussels with chilli-lime
sauce (page 25)

samosas with tamarind sauce

PREPARATION TIME 40 MINUTES (PLUS COOLING TIME)
COOKING TIME 30 MINUTES

1 small brown onion (80g), chopped finely
1 clove garlic, crushed
2 teaspoons ground cumin
1 tablespoon medium curry paste
300g lamb mince
2 tablespoons finely chopped fresh coriander
1 small kumara (250g), chopped finely
1/4 cup (60ml) chicken stock
1 tablespoon lime juice
1/4 cup (30g) frozen peas
3 sheets ready-rolled shortcrust pastry
1 egg, beaten lightly
2 tablespoons tamarind paste
2 tablespoons finely chopped fresh lemon grass
2 tablespoons finely grated palm sugar
1/3 cup (80ml) orange juice

DO AHEAD Unbaked filled samosas can be prepared up to a month ahead and frozen in an airtight container. Samosa filling and tamarind sauce can be prepared a day ahead. Cover separately; refrigerate until required.

1 Cook onion, garlic, cumin and curry paste in medium frying pan, stirring, until onion softens. Add lamb; cook, stirring, until lamb changes colour. Stir in coriander, kumara, stock and lime juice; bring to a boil. Reduce heat; simmer, uncovered, until kumara softens. Stir in peas; simmer, uncovered, until most of the liquid has evaporated. Cool.
2 Preheat oven to moderately hot. Lightly oil two oven trays.
3 Cut each pastry sheet into 16 squares. Divide lamb mixture among squares, brushing edges with a little egg. Bring four corners of each square together in centre, pressing together to enclose filling.
4 Place samosas on prepared trays; brush tops with remaining egg. Bake, uncovered, in moderately hot oven about 15 minutes or until browned lightly.
5 Meanwhile, combine remaining ingredients in small saucepan; cook, stirring, over low heat until tamarind sauce is smooth.
6 Serve hot samosas with tamarind sauce.

makes 48
per samosa 3.6g fat; 267kJ (64 cal)
per tablespoon tamarind sauce 0.3g fat; 104kJ (25 cal)

goes well with
tikka prawns with raita (page 60)
tandoori chicken on naan (page 53)

tarragon and lime scallops

PREPARATION TIME 15 MINUTES **COOKING TIME** 10 MINUTES

DO AHEAD Uncooked scallops and lime wedges can be skewered up to 4 hours ahead. Cover; refrigerate until required.

You need 24 bamboo skewers for this recipe; soak them in cold water for at least an hour prior to use to prevent splintering or scorching.

24 scallops, without roe (500g)
2 tablespoons coarsely
    chopped fresh tarragon
1 tablespoon lime juice
1 tablespoon olive oil
3 limes

1 Rinse scallops under cold water; dry with absorbent paper. Combine scallops in medium bowl with tarragon, juice and oil; toss to coat scallops all over.
2 Cut each lime into eight wedges. Thread one scallop and one lime wedge on each skewer. Cook, in batches, on heated oiled grill plate (or grill or barbecue) until scallops are cooked through.
3 Serve hot.

makes 24
per skewer 0.9g fat;
83kJ (20 cal)

goes well with
salmon tartare (page 22)
greek mini pizzas (page 115)

chorizo taquitos with chilli tomato salsa

PREPARATION TIME 40 MINUTES **COOKING TIME** 15 MINUTES

DO AHEAD Taquito filling and chilli tomato salsa can be prepared a day ahead. Cover separately; refrigerate until required.

You need 40 toothpicks with two-pointed ends for this recipe.

450g can refried beans
1 tablespoon water
400g chorizo sausage,
   chopped finely
1/2 medium red capsicum
   (100g), chopped finely
3 green onions, chopped finely
10 large flour tortillas, quartered
vegetable oil, for deep-frying
CHUNKY TOMATO SALSA
425g can peeled tomatoes
2 red thai chillies,
   seeded, quartered
1 clove garlic, quartered
1/3 cup loosely packed
   fresh coriander leaves
1 small brown onion
   (80g), quartered

1 Heat beans with the water
   in small saucepan.
2 Meanwhile, cook chorizo in
   large non-stick frying pan,
   stirring, until crisp; drain on
   absorbent paper.
3 Combine bean mixture and
   chorizo in medium bowl with
   capsicum and onion. Divide
   filling among tortilla pieces; roll
   each taquito into cone shape,
   secure with toothpick.
4 Heat oil in large saucepan;
   deep-fry taquitos, in batches,
   until browned lightly and crisp.
   Drain on absorbent paper.
   Remove toothpicks.
5 Serve hot taquitos with salsa.
   CHUNKY TOMATO SALSA
   Blend or process ingredients
   until just combined.

makes 40
per taquito 5.2g fat; 337kJ (80 cal)
per tablespoon salsa 0g fat; 17kJ (4 cal)

goes well with
chile con queso (page 106)
polenta carnitas with salsa cruda (page 96)

curry puffs with chutney dip

PREPARATION TIME 40 MINUTES **COOKING TIME** 25 MINUTES

1 tablespoon vegetable oil

2 green onions, chopped finely

1 clove garlic, crushed

2 teaspoons curry powder

300g beef mince

2 teaspoons lemon juice

1/3 cup (110g) mango chutney

4 sheets ready-rolled puff pastry

1 egg, beaten lightly

CHUTNEY DIP

2/3 cup (220g) mango chutney

1 tablespoon water

DO AHEAD Unbaked filled curry puffs can be prepared up to a month ahead and frozen in an airtight container. Curry puff filling and chutney dip can be prepared a day ahead. Cover separately; refrigerate until required.

1 Heat oil in medium saucepan; cook onion and garlic, stirring, until onion softens. Add curry powder; cook, stirring, until fragrant. Add beef; cook, stirring, until beef is browned and cooked through. Remove from heat; stir in juice and chutney.

2 Using rolling pin, roll each pastry sheet into 30cm square. Using 8cm-round cutter, cut eight rounds from each pastry sheet.

3 Preheat oven to moderately hot. Lightly oil two oven trays.

4 Place one heaped teaspoon of the beef mixture on one round; brush edges with a little egg, fold over to enclose filling. Press edges with fork to seal; repeat with remaining beef mixture and pastry.

5 Place curry puffs on prepared oven trays; brush with remaining egg. Bake, uncovered, in moderately hot oven about 15 minutes or until browned lightly.

6 Serve hot with warm chutney dip.

CHUTNEY DIP Combine ingredients in small saucepan; stir over low heat until combined.

makes 32

per curry puff 6.2g fat; 439kJ (105 cal)

per tablespoon chutney 0.1g fat; 179kJ (43 cal)

goes well with

samosas with tamarind sauce (page 68)

tandoori chicken on naan (page 53)

fried ravioli bolognese

PREPARATION TIME 30 MINUTES (PLUS COOLING TIME) **COOKING TIME** 45 MINUTES

DO AHEAD Bolognese filling can be prepared a day ahead. Cover; refrigerate until required.

1 tablespoon olive oil
1 small brown onion (80g),
  chopped finely
1 clove garlic, crushed
100g mushrooms,
  chopped finely
300g beef mince
3/4 cup (180ml) tomato puree
3/4 cup (180ml) beef stock
1/4 cup (60ml) dry red wine
32 wonton wrappers
vegetable oil, for deep-frying

1 Heat olive oil in medium frying pan; cook onion and garlic, stirring, until onion softens. Add mushrooms; cook, stirring, until mushrooms soften. Add beef; cook, stirring, until beef changes colour. Add puree, stock and wine; bring to a boil. Reduce heat; simmer, uncovered, 20 minutes or until liquid is almost evaporated. Cool.
2 Place rounded teaspoons of the bolognese in centre of wrappers. Brush edges with a little water; pinch edges together to seal. Cut edges of wrappers with fluted pastry cutter, if desired.
3 Heat vegetable oil in large saucepan; deep-fry ravioli, in batches, until golden brown, drain on absorbent paper.
4 Serve hot.

makes 32
per ravioli 3.2g fat; 209kJ (50 cal)

goes well with
bruschetta niçoise (page 28)
bocconcini, olive and
cherry tomato skewers
with pesto (page 34)

beef wontons

PREPARATION TIME 45 MINUTES (PLUS COOLING TIME)   **COOKING TIME** 30 MINUTES

DO AHEAD Uncooked wontons can be prepared up to 4 hours ahead. Cover; refrigerate until required.

1 tablespoon sesame oil
400g lean beef mince
190g can water chestnut slices,
   drained, chopped finely
1 tablespoon light soy sauce
1 tablespoon oyster sauce
1 tablespoon sesame seeds
40 wonton wrappers
1 egg white, beaten lightly
vegetable oil, for shallow-frying

1   Heat sesame oil in medium
    frying pan; cook beef, stirring,
    until browned and cooked
    through. Remove from heat;
    stir in water chestnut, sauces
    and seeds. Cool in pan.
2   Place rounded teaspoons of
    the beef mixture in centre of
    wrappers; brush edges with a
    little egg white. Fold wrappers
    in half diagonally; pinch edges
    together to seal.
3   Heat vegetable oil in large frying
    pan; shallow-fry wontons, in
    batches, until browned both
    sides, drain on absorbent paper.
4   Serve hot with a bowl of
    sweet chilli sauce.

makes 40
per wonton 3.7g fat;
222kJ (53 cal)

goes well with
*vietnamese rice paper
rolls (page 14)
oven-baked spring rolls
(page 100)*

prawn dumplings

PREPARATION TIME 40 MINUTES **COOKING TIME** 10 MINUTES

DO AHEAD Uncooked dumplings can be prepared up to 4 hours ahead. Cover; refrigerate until required.

1kg uncooked prawns
¼ cup (50g) bamboo shoots,
   chopped finely
1 tablespoon finely
   chopped fresh chives
2 teaspoons sesame oil
2 teaspoons cornflour
24 gow gee wrappers

1 Shell and devein prawns; chop finely. Combine prawns in large bowl with bamboo shoots, chives, oil and cornflour. Blend or process half of the prawn mixture until just smooth. Return to large bowl with remaining prawn mixture; stir to combine.

2 Place one wrapper on your hand; place one heaped teaspoon of the prawn mixture into centre of wrapper. Gently cup your hand and gather sides of wrapper to form pleats, leaving top open. Press base of wrapper on bench to flatten. Repeat with remaining wrappers and prawn mixture.

3 Place dumplings, without touching, in lightly oiled steamer; steam, in batches, over large saucepan of boiling water 10 minutes.

4 Serve hot with light soy sauce.

makes 24
per dumpling 0.5g fat;
135kJ (32 cal)

goes well with
chicken yakitori with sesame dipping sauce (page 92)
smoked trout on crispy wonton wrappers (page 17)

peanut and chicken gow gees

PREPARATION TIME 30 MINUTES (PLUS STANDING TIME) **COOKING TIME** 20 MINUTES

DO AHEAD Uncooked gow gees can be prepared up to 4 hours ahead. Cover; refrigerate until required.

3 dried shiitake mushrooms
1 trimmed stick celery (75g),
  chopped finely
1 tablespoon finely chopped,
  unsalted, roasted peanuts
1 clove garlic, crushed
1 green onion, chopped finely
2 teaspoons hoisin sauce
200g chicken mince
40 gow gee wrappers
DIPPING SAUCE
¼ cup (60ml) kecap manis
2 teaspoons red wine vinegar

1 Place mushrooms in small
  heatproof bowl, cover with
  boiling water; stand 20 minutes,
  drain. Discard stems; chop
  caps finely.
2 Combine mushrooms in medium
  bowl with celery, nuts, garlic,
  onion, sauce and chicken.
3 Place one heaped teaspoon of
  the chicken mixture in centre
  of one wrapper; brush around
  half of the wrapper's edge with
  a little water. Pleat damp side
  of wrapper only; pinch both
  sides together to seal. Repeat
  with remaining chicken mixture
  and wrappers.
4 Poach gow gees, in batches,
  in large saucepan of boiling
  water about 5 minutes or until
  cooked through.
5 Serve hot with dipping sauce.
  DIPPING SAUCE Combine
  ingredients in small bowl.

makes 40
per gow gee 0.6g fat;
82kJ (20 cal)
per tablespoon sauce 0g fat;
35kJ (8 cal)

goes well with
pork satay (page 93)
peking duck wraps (page 16)

gorgonzola and fennel tartlets

PREPARATION TIME 20 MINUTES **COOKING TIME** 20 MINUTES

DO AHEAD Fennel mixture can be cooked a day ahead. Cover; refrigerate until required.

You need two 12-hole mini (1¹/₂ tablespoons/30ml) muffin pans for this recipe.

120g gorgonzola cheese, crumbled
¹/₂ cup (120g) sour cream
2 eggs
1 tablespoon olive oil
2 small fennel (600g), trimmed, halved, sliced thinly
4 sheets fillo pastry
cooking-oil spray

1 Blend or process cheese, sour cream and eggs until smooth; transfer to large jug.
2 Heat oil in small frying pan; cook fennel, stirring, until soft.
3 Preheat oven to moderate. Lightly oil two 12-hole mini muffin pans.
4 Cut pastry into 7cm squares. Stack two squares of pastry on board; spray with oil. Place another two squares diagonally on top to make star shape; spray with oil. Press into hole of mini muffin pan; repeat with remaining pastry.
5 Divide cheese mixture among pastry cases; top with fennel. Bake, uncovered, in moderate oven about 15 minutes or until filling sets and pastry is browned lightly. Stand tartlets in pans 5 minutes.
6 Serve hot.

makes 24
per tartlet 5g fat; 254kJ (61 cal)

goes well with
mushroom and herb palmiers (page 113)
pecan chicken salad finger sandwiches (page 54)

CHICKEN WINGS

Wings can be cooked the day before required. Cover; refrigerate until required. To reheat, place wings in single layer on oven tray, cover with foil; bake in preheated hot oven for about 10 minutes.

classic buffalo wings

PREPARATION TIME 15 MINUTES
(PLUS REFRIGERATION TIME)
COOKING TIME 15 MINUTES

16 small chicken wings (1.3kg)
vegetable oil, for deep-frying
1/3 cup (80ml) hot chilli sauce
80g butter, melted
1/2 cup (150g) mayonnaise
1/2 cup (120g) sour cream
1/4 cup (60ml) buttermilk
2 teaspoons lemon juice
1/4 teaspoon hot paprika
1 small brown onion (80g), chopped coarsely
100g danish blue cheese, crumbled
4 trimmed sticks celery (300g), cut into sticks

1 Cut wings into three pieces at joints; discard tips. Heat oil in large saucepan; deep-fry chicken, in batches, until cooked through, drain. Combine chicken in large bowl with sauce and butter.
2 Blend mayonnaise, sour cream, milk, juice, paprika, onion and half of the cheese until smooth; stir in remaining cheese. Cover; refrigerate 2 hours.
3 Serve hot with blue cheese sauce and celery sticks.

makes 32
per wing 8.9g fat; 481kJ (115 cal)

honey soy wings

PREPARATION TIME 10 MINUTES
COOKING TIME 30 MINUTES

16 small chicken wings (1.3kg)
1/3 cup (115g) honey
1/2 cup (125ml) salt-reduced soy sauce
3 cloves garlic, crushed
1 tablespoon grated fresh ginger

1 Preheat oven to hot.
2 Cut wings into three pieces at joints; discard tips. Combine chicken with remaining ingredients in large bowl; toss to coat chicken all over.
3 Place chicken, in single layer, in large shallow baking dish; brush any remaining marinade over chicken. Bake, uncovered, in hot oven, turning occasionally, about 30 minutes or until chicken is browned and cooked through.
4 Serve hot.

makes 32
per wing 1.4g fat; 205kJ (49 cal)

TIP Wing tips can be used to make chicken stock.

spicy wings with apricot mustard sauce

PREPARATION TIME 20 MINUTES
COOKING TIME 15 MINUTES

16 small chicken wings (1.3kg)
1/2 cup (75g) plain flour
2 eggs, beaten lightly
1/4 cup (60ml) milk
2 1/2 cups (250g) packaged breadcrumbs
1 tablespoon dried chilli flakes
vegetable oil, for deep-frying
1 cup (320g) apricot jam
2 tablespoons dijon mustard
2 teaspoons light soy sauce
1 clove garlic, crushed

1 Cut wings into three pieces at joints; discard tips. Coat chicken in flour, shake away excess; dip chicken into combined egg and milk, then into combined breadcrumbs and chilli.
2 Heat oil in large saucepan; deep-fry chicken, in batches, until browned and cooked through, drain.
3 Blend or process remaining ingredients until smooth.
4 Serve hot with apricot mustard sauce.

makes 32
per wing 4.3g fat; 518kJ (124 cal)

lime and soy wings

PREPARATION TIME 20 MINUTES
(PLUS REFRIGERATION TIME)
COOKING TIME 25 MINUTES

16 small chicken wings (1.3 kg)
3/4 cup (240g) lime marmalade, warmed
1/2 cup (125ml) light soy sauce
1/4 cup (60ml) dry white wine
1 clove garlic, crushed
1/3 cup (80ml) barbecue sauce
1 tablespoon lime juice

1 Cut wings into three pieces at joints; discard tips.
2 Combine marmalade, sauce, wine and garlic in large bowl. Add chicken; toss to coat chicken all over. Cover; refrigerate 3 hours or overnight.
3 Cook drained chicken, in batches, on heated oiled grill plate (or grill or barbecue), brushing both sides occasionally with barbecue sauce, about 25 minutes or until chicken is cooked through.
4 Serve hot drizzled with lime juice.

makes 32
per wing 1.4g fat; 260kJ (62 cal)

Tiny new potatoes make the perfect base for any number of delectable savoury hors d'oeuvres. Here are three of our favourite filling recipes to start you on your way. Each filling recipe makes enough for 24 tiny new potatoes.

baby potato bites

PREPARATION TIME 15 MINUTES (PLUS COOLING TIME)
COOKING TIME 15 MINUTES

DO AHEAD Potatoes can be cooked (but not hollowed out) on the day before serving. Cover; refrigerate until required.

24 tiny new potatoes (960g)
1 portion of any of the 3 fillings at right

1 Boil, steam or microwave potatoes until just tender; drain. Cool.
2 Preheat oven to moderately hot.
3 Cut shallow slice from top of each potato; using a melon-baller, carefully scoop out about two-thirds of the flesh of each potato. Reserve flesh.
4 Divide filling among hollowed-out potatoes, as instructed in each recipe. Place potatoes on oiled oven tray. Bake, uncovered, in moderately hot oven about 15 minutes or until heated through.
5 Serve hot.

pea puree

PREPARATION TIME 10 MINUTES
COOKING TIME 20 MINUTES

DO AHEAD Filling can be made a day ahead. Cover; refrigerate until required.

1²/3 cups (200g) frozen peas
40g butter, chopped
¹/3 cup (25g) finely grated parmesan cheese

1 Boil, steam or microwave peas until just tender; drain.
2 Blend or process peas with reserved potato flesh and butter until pureed; stir in ¹/4 cup of the cheese.
3 Spoon filling into potatoes, sprinkle with remaining cheese. Proceed as instructed in baby potato bites recipe.

makes 24
per potato 1.8g fat; 200kJ (48 cal)

pancetta and gruyère

PREPARATION TIME 15 MINUTES
COOKING TIME 25 MINUTES

DO AHEAD Filling can be made a day ahead.
Cover; refrigerate until required.

150g pancetta
20g butter
1 tablespoon wholegrain mustard
1/3 cup (40g) finely grated gruyère cheese
1/3 cup (80g) sour cream
2 tablespoons finely chopped fresh chives

1 Cook pancetta, in batches, in large heated
   frying pan until crisp; drain on absorbent paper,
   chop finely.
2 Mash reserved potato flesh in medium bowl with
   butter, mustard, cheese and sour cream; stir in
   half of the pancetta and half of the chives.
3 Spoon filling into potatoes; sprinkle with remaining
   pancetta. Proceed as instructed in baby potato bites
   recipe; sprinkle with remaining chives after baking.

makes 24
per potato 2.7g fat; 241kJ (58 cal)

chicken and corn

PREPARATION TIME 15 MINUTES
COOKING TIME 15 MINUTES

DO AHEAD Filling can be made a day ahead.
Cover; refrigerate until required.

You need to purchase a small barbecued chicken
for this recipe. Remove and discard the chicken
skin and bones before chopping the meat; reserve
any leftover meat for another use.

1 1/2 cups (240g) finely chopped barbecued chicken
125g can creamed corn
2 tablespoons sour cream
3 green onions, chopped finely
1/4 cup (20g) finely grated parmesan cheese

1 Combine reserved potato flesh and remaining
   ingredients in medium bowl.
2 Spoon filling into potatoes. Proceed as instructed
   in baby potato bites recipe.

makes 24
per potato 1.8g fat; 244kJ (58 cal)

cottage pies

PREPARATION TIME 25 MINUTES **COOKING TIME** 30 MINUTES

DO AHEAD Beef filling and mash can be prepared a day ahead. Cover separately; refrigerate until required.

You need to purchase 48 baked 4cm tartlet cases for this recipe.

3 medium potatoes (600g), chopped coarsely
1 tablespoon olive oil
1 medium brown onion (150g), chopped finely
2 cloves garlic, crushed
250g beef mince
1 cup (250ml) tomato puree
1/3 cup (80ml) dry red wine
2 tablespoons worcestershire sauce
1 tablespoon fresh thyme leaves
1/4 cup (30g) frozen peas
2 tablespoons finely chopped fresh flat-leaf parsley
1/4 cup (60g) sour cream
1 egg yolk
48 x 4cm tartlet cases

1 Boil, steam or microwave potato until tender; drain.
2 Meanwhile, heat oil in large frying pan; cook onion and garlic until onion softens. Add beef; cook, stirring, until beef changes colour. Stir in puree, wine, sauce and thyme; bring to a boil. Reduce heat; simmer, uncovered, about 15 minutes or until almost all liquid has evaporated. Stir in peas and parsley.
3 Mash potato in large bowl with sour cream and egg yolk until combined. Spoon potato mixture into piping bag fitted with large fluted tube.
4 Place pastry cases on oven trays. Divide beef mixture among cases; pipe potato over beef. Grill pies about 5 minutes or until tops brown and pies are heated through.
5 Serve hot.

makes 48
per pie 2g fat; 164kJ (39 cal)

goes well with
mini prawn cocktails (page 32)
filet mignons with béarnaise sauce (page 104)

gyoza with soy vinegar sauce

PREPARATION TIME 40 MINUTES (PLUS REFRIGERATION TIME) **COOKING TIME** 15 MINUTES

DO AHEAD Gyoza filling can be prepared up to 4 hours ahead. Cover; refrigerate until required.

300g pork mince
2 tablespoons kecap manis
1 teaspoon sugar
1 tablespoon sake
1 egg, beaten lightly
2 teaspoons sesame oil
3 cups (240g) finely shredded
 chinese cabbage
4 green onions, sliced thinly
40 gyoza or gow gee wrappers
1 tablespoon vegetable oil
SOY VINEGAR SAUCE
½ cup (125ml) light soy sauce
¼ cup (60ml) red vinegar
2 tablespoons white vinegar
2 tablespoons sweet
 chilli sauce

1 Combine pork, kecap manis, sugar, sake, egg, sesame oil, cabbage and onion in large bowl; refrigerate 1 hour.

2 Place one heaped teaspoon of the pork mixture in centre of one wrapper; brush one edge of wrapper with a little water. Pleat damp side of wrapper only; pinch both sides together to seal. Repeat with remaining pork mixture and wrappers.

3 Cover base of large frying pan with water; bring to a boil. Add dumplings, in batches; reduce heat, simmer, covered, 3 minutes. Using slotted spoon, remove dumplings from pan. Drain pan; dry thoroughly.

4 Heat vegetable oil in same pan; cook dumplings, in batches, unpleated side and base only, until golden brown.

5 Serve hot with soy vinegar sauce.
SOY VINEGAR SAUCE Combine ingredients in small bowl.

makes 40
per gyoza 1.4g fat; 139kJ (31 cal)
per tablespoon sauce 0.1g fat; 35kJ (8 cal)

goes well with
rumaki (page 107)
oysters osaka (page 21)

oysters with pesto butter

PREPARATION TIME 10 MINUTES (PLUS REFRIGERATION TIME) **COOKING TIME** 5 MINUTES

DO AHEAD Pesto butter can be prepared up to 3 days ahead. Cover; refrigerate until required.

125g butter, softened
1 tablespoon lemon juice
2 tablespoons coarsely
   chopped fresh basil
2 tablespoons pine nuts,
   toasted
24 oysters, on the half shell

1 Blend or process butter, juice
   and basil until smooth; fold in
   nuts. Cover; refrigerate until firm.
2 Preheat oven to moderately hot.
3 Divide pesto butter among
   oysters. Bake, uncovered,
   in moderately hot oven about
   5 minutes or until butter melts
   and oysters are heated through.
4 Serve hot.

makes 24
per oyster 5.4g fat;
225kJ (54 cal)

goes well with
radicchio with thai crab
salad (page 18)
risotto-filled zucchini flowers
(page 110)

yorkshire puddings with gravy

PREPARATION TIME 10 MINUTES **COOKING TIME** 10 MINUTES

Traditionally, beef dripping is used in making yorkshire puddings, but for this quick and easy finger-food version, we use equal amounts of vegetable oil and butter. If you prefer, however, you can replace the oil and butter combination with all lard or all dripping, both of which can be found in your supermarket's refrigerated section where butter is sold. You need two 12-hole mini (1 1/2 tablespoons/30ml) muffin pans for this recipe.

2 eggs
2/3 cup (160ml) milk
2/3 cup (100g) plain flour
2 tablespoons vegetable oil
40g butter
1/4 cup (35g) plain flour, extra
1 cup (250ml) beef stock
1/3 cup (80ml) water
1 tablespoon light soy sauce

1 Preheat oven to very hot.
2 Whisk eggs, milk and flour in medium bowl until smooth.
3 Heat oil and butter in small saucepan over low heat until butter melts. Pour half of the oil mixture into small jug; reserve remaining half in pan.
4 Divide oil mixture in jug among holes of two 12-hole mini muffin pans. Place in very hot oven about 1 minute or until oil mixture is very hot.
5 Working quickly, divide batter among holes of pans. Bake, uncovered, in very hot oven about 10 minutes or until puddings rise and are browned lightly.
6 Meanwhile, reheat oil mixture in pan; add extra flour, cook, stirring, about 4 minutes or until mixture thickens and bubbles. Gradually add combined stock and the water, stirring, until gravy boils and thickens. Stir in sauce.
7 Serve hot with gravy.

makes 24
per pudding 2.3g fat; 162kJ (39 cal)
per tablespoon gravy 2.7g fat; 134kJ (32 cal)

goes well with
prawn remoulade (page 20)
filet mignons with béarnaise sauce (page 104)

mussel kebabs with walnut sauce

PREPARATION TIME 10 MINUTES **COOKING TIME** 10 MINUTES

DO AHEAD Uncooked mussels can be skewered and sauce made up to 3 hours ahead. Cover separately; refrigerate until required.

You need 16 bamboo skewers for this recipe; soak them in cold water for at least an hour to prevent splintering or scorching.

48 large mussels (1.3kg)
½ cup (110g) plain flour
¾ cup (180ml) water
vegetable oil, for deep-frying
¾ cup (75g) walnuts, toasted
2 cloves garlic, crushed
¾ cup (45g) stale breadcrumbs
2 tablespoons olive oil
1 tablespoon white
   wine vinegar
¼ cup (60ml) lemon juice
1 tablespoon water, extra

1 Scrub mussels under cold water; remove beards. Boil, steam or microwave mussels until shells open (discard any that do not); cool. Using spoon, gently remove mussels from shells; discard shells. Thread three mussels on each skewer.
2 Blend flour with the water in medium bowl; whisk until batter is smooth.
3 Heat oil in medium saucepan; dip kebabs in batter; deep-fry, in batches, until browned lightly. Drain on absorbent paper.
4 Meanwhile, blend or process nuts, garlic and breadcrumbs until combined. With motor operating, gradually pour in combined oil, vinegar, juice and the extra water; blend until sauce is smooth.
5 Serve mussel kebabs hot with walnut sauce.

goes well with
scallops st jacques-style
(page 109)
profiteroles with salmon mousse
(page 36)

makes 16
per kebab 2.1g fat;
220kJ (53 cal)
per tablespoon sauce
7.7g fat; 359kJ (86 cal)

grilled lamb cutlets with tomato compote

PREPARATION TIME 10 MINUTES **COOKING TIME** 30 MINUTES

DO AHEAD Cutlets can be coated in sumac and compote made a day ahead. Cover separately; refrigerate until required.

40 lamb cutlets (3kg)
1 tablespoon sumac
1 tablespoon olive oil
1 large brown onion (200g), chopped finely
2 cloves garlic, crushed
2 x 415g cans crushed tomatoes
½ cup (125ml) dry red wine
1 tablespoon balsamic vinegar

1 Trim fat from lamb. Place sumac and lamb in large bowl; toss to coat lamb all over. Reserve.
2 Heat oil in medium saucepan; cook onion and garlic, stirring, until onion softens. Add remaining ingredients; bring to a boil. Reduce heat; simmer, uncovered, about 25 minutes or until liquid is almost evaporated.
3 Cook lamb, in batches, on heated oiled grill plate (or grill or barbecue) until browned both sides and cooked as desired.
4 Serve hot with tomato compote.

makes 40
per cutlet 3.5g fat;
274kJ (66 cal)
per tablespoon compote
0.5g fat; 47kJ (11 cal)

goes well with
prawn remoulade (page 20)
pea puree potato bites
(page 82)

Sumac is a purple-red, astringent spice, ground from berries growing on shrubs around the eastern Mediterranean. It adds a tart, lemony flavour to the lamb. It is available at Middle-Eastern or Asian food stores.

chicken yakitori with sesame dipping sauce

PREPARATION TIME 20 MINUTES **COOKING TIME** 10 MINUTES

DO AHEAD The uncooked chicken can be skewered and sauce made a day ahead. Cover separately; refrigerate until required.

You need 32 bamboo skewers for this recipe; soak them in cold water for at least an hour to prevent splintering or scorching.

1kg chicken breast fillets
¼ cup (60ml) light soy sauce
2 tablespoons mirin
3 teaspoons sugar
½ teaspoon sesame oil
1 teaspoon sesame seeds

1 Cut chicken into 32 long thin slices; thread each slice on a skewer. Cook, in batches, on heated oiled grill plate (or grill or barbecue) until chicken is browned all over and cooked through.
2 Meanwhile, combine remaining ingredients in small bowl.
3 Serve chicken hot with sauce.

makes 32
per yakitori 1.7g fat;
177kJ (42 cal)
per tablespoon sauce
0.6g fat; 107kJ (25 cal)

goes well with
chicken teriyaki
mini maki (page 49)
gyoza with soy vinegar
sauce (page 86)

pork satay

PREPARATION TIME 25 MINUTES **COOKING TIME** 10 MINUTES

DO AHEAD Uncooked pork can be skewered and sauce made a day ahead. Cover separately; refrigerate until required.

You need 32 bamboo skewers for this recipe; soak them in cold water for at least an hour to prevent splintering or scorching.

1kg pork fillets
¼ cup (60ml) olive oil
1 teaspoon freshly ground
   black pepper
½ cup (140g) crunchy
   peanut butter
¼ cup (60ml) sweet chilli sauce
1 clove garlic, crushed
1 cup (250ml) chicken stock
¼ cup (35g) coconut
   milk powder

1 Cut pork into 32 x 8cm strips; thread each strip on a skewer.
2 Brush with combined oil and pepper. Cook, in batches, on heated oiled grill plate (or grill or barbecue) until pork is browned all over and cooked as desired.
3 Meanwhile, combine remaining ingredients in small saucepan; bring to a boil. Reduce heat; simmer, uncovered, 2 minutes or until sauce thickens slightly.
4 Serve pork hot with satay sauce.

makes 32
per skewer 2.4g fat;
206kJ (49 cal)
per tablespoon sauce
5.3g fat; 265kJ (63 cal)

goes well with
thai coconut prawns (page 61)
thai chicken salad in crispy
wonton cups (page 26)

sausage rolls

PREPARATION TIME 15 MINUTES **COOKING TIME** 20 MINUTES

DO AHEAD Sausage roll filling can be prepared a day ahead. Cover; refrigerate until required.

1 tablespoon vegetable oil
1 medium brown onion (150g),
  chopped finely
3 slices white bread,
  crusts removed
350g sausage mince
350g beef mince
1 tablespoon tomato paste
1 teaspoon dried mixed herbs
2 tablespoons finely chopped
  fresh flat-leaf parsley
4 sheets ready-rolled puff pastry
1 egg, beaten lightly
2 tablespoons sesame seeds

1 Heat oil in small frying pan; cook
   onion until soft. Dip bread in
   small bowl of cold water; remove
   immediately, discard water.
2 Combine onion and bread in
   large bowl with minces, paste,
   mixed herbs and parsley.
3 Preheat oven to hot. Lightly oil
   two oven trays.
4 Cut pastry sheets in half
   lengthways. Place equal amounts
   of filling mixture lengthways along
   centre of each pastry piece; roll
   each pastry piece, from one wide
   edge, to enclose filling. Place four
   rolls, seam-side down, on each of
   the prepared trays; brush with egg.
   Sprinkle with sesame seeds; cut
   each roll into eight pieces. Bake,
   uncovered, in hot oven about
   15 minutes or until browned.
5 Serve hot with tomato sauce.

makes 64
per roll 4.7g fat; 296kJ (71 cal)

goes well with
liptauer (page 13)
lamb and rocket mini
pizzas (page 114)

deep-fried onion rings

PREPARATION TIME 20 MINUTES **COOKING TIME** 20 MINUTES

DO AHEAD Dipping sauce can be made a day ahead. Cover; refrigerate until required.

½ cup (75g) plain flour
½ cup (75g) cornflour
1 egg, beaten lightly
¾ cup (180ml) water
1½ cups (150g) packaged
   breadcrumbs
2 large white onions (400g),
   sliced thickly
vegetable oil, for deep-frying
SWEET CHILLI DIPPING SAUCE
½ cup (120g) sour cream
¼ cup (60ml) sweet chilli sauce
2 tablespoons cream

1   Whisk flour, cornflour, egg
    and the water in medium
    bowl until smooth; place
    breadcrumbs in small bowl.
2   Separate onion slices into
    rings. Dip rings, one at a time,
    in batter, then in breadcrumbs
    to coat; place, in single layer,
    on tray until all rings are coated.
3   Heat oil in large saucepan;
    deep-fry rings, in batches,
    until golden brown, drain on
    absorbent paper.
4   Serve hot with sweet chilli
    dipping sauce.
    SWEET CHILLI DIPPING SAUCE
    Combine sour cream, sauce
    and cream in small bowl.

makes 64
per onion ring
0.9g fat; 109kJ (26 cal)
per tablespoon sauce
6.1g fat; 258kJ (62 cal)

goes well with
cheeseburgers (page 64)
BLT on mini toasts (page 52)

polenta carnitas with salsa cruda

PREPARATION TIME 45 MINUTES (PLUS REFRIGERATION TIME) **COOKING TIME** 1 HOUR 15 MINUTES

2 cups (500ml) water
1/2 cup (125ml) vegetable stock
1 cup (250ml) milk
1 1/2 cups (255g) polenta
20g butter
3/4 cup (60g) finely grated parmesan cheese
150g diced pork
1/2 teaspoon chilli powder
4 black peppercorns
1 clove garlic
1 cup (250ml) water, extra
cooking-oil spray
1/2 cup (120g) sour cream
SALSA CRUDA
1 medium tomato (190g), seeded, chopped finely
1 small white onion (80g), chopped finely
2 tablespoons finely chopped fresh coriander
2 fresh red thai chillies, seeded, chopped finely
1 tablespoon lime juice

DO AHEAD Unbaked cooked polenta and shredded pork can be prepared, and salsa made, a day ahead. Cover separately; refrigerate until required.

Carnitas, "little meats" in Spanish, are a famous Mexican pork snack, usually served with an uncooked fresh tomato and chilli sauce called salsa cruda.

1 Lightly oil 20cm x 30cm lamington pan.
2 Heat the water, stock and milk in large saucepan (do not boil). Add polenta; cook, stirring, about 5 minutes or until polenta thickens. Stir in butter and cheese. Spoon polenta into prepared pan; press firmly to ensure even thickness. Cool. Cover; refrigerate about 3 hours or until firm.
3 Meanwhile, combine pork, chilli powder, peppercorns, garlic and the extra water in medium saucepan; bring to a boil. Reduce heat; simmer, covered, about 45 minutes or until pork is tender. Cool in liquid.
4 Drain pork, discard peppercorns; shred pork finely.
5 Preheat oven to very hot.
6 Turn polenta onto board; trim edges. Cut into 3cm x 4cm pieces. Place on oiled oven tray; spray with oil. Bake, uncovered, in very hot oven about 10 minutes or until crisp and browned lightly both sides. Divide salsa cruda, shredded pork and sour cream among polenta pieces.
7 Serve hot.
SALSA CRUDA Combine ingredients in small bowl.

makes 40
per carnita 2.7g fat; 219kJ (52 cal)
per tablespoon salsa 0g fat; 10kJ (2 cal)

goes well with
chile con queso (page 106)
bloody mary oyster shots (page 24)

deep-fried mozzarella sticks

PREPARATION TIME 10 MINUTES **COOKING TIME** 10 MINUTES

DO AHEAD Mozzarella can be cut into sticks and sauce made a day ahead. Cover separately; refrigerate until required.

1 cup (150g) plain flour
1 cup (150g) cornflour
2 eggs, beaten lightly
1½ cups (375ml) water
1 cup (100g) packaged
  breadcrumbs
500g mozzarella
vegetable oil, for deep-frying
CHILLI PESTO DIPPING SAUCE
⅓ cup (90g) sun-dried
  tomato pesto
⅔ cup (160ml) sweet
  chilli sauce

1 Whisk flour, cornflour, egg and the water in medium bowl until smooth; place breadcrumbs in small bowl.
2 Cut cheese into 1cm-wide fingers.
3 Dip cheese sticks, one at a time, in batter, then in breadcrumbs to coat. Dip cheese sticks, one at a time, back in batter, then in breadcrumbs to double-coat.
4 Heat oil in large saucepan; deep-fry cheese sticks, in batches, until golden brown, drain on absorbent paper.
5 Serve hot with chilli pesto dipping sauce.
   CHILLI PESTO DIPPING SAUCE Combine pesto and sauce in small bowl.

MAKES 32
per stick 6.1g fat;
479kJ (114 cal)
per tablespoon sauce
3.4g fat; 188kJ (45 cal)

goes well with
mini zucchini frittatas (page 38)
lamb and rocket mini
pizzas (page 114)

spicy lamb and pine nut triangles

PREPARATION TIME 30 MINUTES **COOKING TIME** 30 MINUTES

DO AHEAD Lamb filling can be cooked up to 2 days ahead. Cover; refrigerate until required.

10g butter
1 medium brown onion (150g),
   chopped finely
1 clove garlic, crushed
1/2 teaspoon ground
   mixed spice
1/2 teaspoon freshly ground
   black pepper
1/2 cup (80g) pine nuts, toasted
2 teaspoons sambal oelek
500g lamb mince
2 green onions, sliced thinly
24 sheets fillo pastry
cooking-oil spray

1   Melt butter in medium non-stick frying pan; cook brown onion, garlic, spice, pepper, nuts and sambal, stirring, until onion softens. Add lamb; cook, stirring, until lamb is browned and cooked through. Stir in green onion.
2   Preheat oven to moderately hot. Lightly oil two oven trays.
3   Spray one pastry sheet with oil, cover with second pastry sheet; cut crossways into six even strips, spray with oil. Repeat with remaining pastry sheets.
4   Place 2 teaspoons of lamb filling on the bottom of narrow edge of one strip, leaving a 1cm border. Fold opposite corner of strip diagonally across filling to form triangle; continue folding to end of strip, retaining triangle shape. Place triangle on prepared tray, seam-side down; repeat with remaining strips and filling. Spray triangles lightly with oil. Bake, uncovered, in moderately hot oven about 10 minutes or until browned lightly.
5   Serve hot.

makes 72
per triangle 1.7g fat; 144kJ (35 cal)

goes well with
smoky eggplant caviar (page 45)
laila's lamb kofta with spiced yogurt (page 58)

oven-baked spring rolls

PREPARATION TIME 30 MINUTES **COOKING TIME** 30 MINUTES

DO AHEAD Pork filling can be cooked and sauce made a day ahead. Cover; refrigerate until required.

goes well with
vietnamese rice paper rolls (page 14)
peanut and chicken gow gees (page 77)

4 dried shiitake mushrooms
1 tablespoon peanut oil
3 green onions, sliced thinly
2 cloves garlic, crushed
450g pork mince
1/3 cup (65g) finely chopped
    water chestnuts
100g chinese cabbage,
    shredded finely
2 teaspoons fish sauce
1 tablespoon light soy sauce
2 tablespoons oyster sauce
48 small spring roll wrappers
1 egg, beaten lightly
CHILLI DIPPING SAUCE
1/3 cup (80ml) chinese
    red wine vinegar
1/3 cup (80ml) sweet chilli sauce

1 Place mushrooms in small heatproof bowl, cover with boiling water; stand 20 minutes, drain. Slice mushrooms thinly.
2 Meanwhile, heat oil in medium wok; stir-fry onion and garlic until onion softens. Add pork; stir-fry until browned and cooked through. Add mushrooms, water chestnuts, cabbage and sauces; stir-fry until cabbage wilts. Cool.
3 Preheat oven to moderately hot. Lightly oil oven trays.
4 Spoon filling onto centre of wrappers; brush edges with egg. Roll each wrapper on the diagonal to enclose filling, folding in sides after first complete turn. Place spring rolls on prepared trays, seam-side down; brush all over with remaining egg. Bake, uncovered, in moderately hot oven about 10 minutes or until browned lightly and crisp.
5 Serve hot with dipping sauce.
CHILLI DIPPING SAUCE Combine ingredients in small bowl.

makes 48
per roll 1.3g fat; 155kJ (37 cal)
per tablespoon sauce
0.3g fat; 54kJ (13 cal)

cheese scones

PREPARATION TIME 10 MINUTES **COOKING TIME** 20 MINUTES

1½ cups (225g)
  self-raising flour
¼ teaspoon ground
  cayenne pepper
2 teaspoons sugar
⅓ cup (25g) finely grated
  parmesan cheese
1 cup (120g) coarsely grated
  cheddar cheese
1 cup (250ml) milk
40g butter, melted
CHIVE BUTTER
60g butter, softened
1 tablespoon finely chopped
  fresh chives

1 Combine flour, cayenne,
  sugar, parmesan and half of
  the cheddar in medium bowl;
  pour in milk, stir until mixture
  makes a sticky dough.
2 Preheat oven to hot. Lightly oil
  and flour 20cm-round pan.
3 Gently knead dough, until smooth,
  on a floured surface. Using one
  hand, flatten dough until about
  an even 2cm-thickness. Using
  3.5cm-round cutter, cut rounds
  from dough. Place rounds, slightly
  touching, in prepared pan.
4 Brush scones with butter; sprinkle
  with remaining cheddar. Bake,
  uncovered, in hot oven about
  20 minutes or until browned
  lightly; turn onto wire rack.
5 Serve warm with chive butter.
  CHIVE BUTTER Combine
  ingredients in small bowl.

makes 24
per scone 6g fat; 398kJ (95 cal)

goes well with
cottage pies (page 84)
mini prawn cocktails (page 32)

chive pancakes with sausages and caramelised onion

PREPARATION TIME 45 MINUTES **COOKING TIME** 45 MINUTES

DO AHEAD Pancakes can be made a day ahead; stack, with small pieces of greaseproof or baking paper separating them, then cover and refrigerate until required.

TIP We used lamb and rosemary sausages; use whichever gourmet sausage you prefer.

goes well with
cream cheese and green olive palmiers (page 113)
blue cheese and green onion mini pizzas (page 115)

¾ cup (110g) self-raising flour
1 teaspoon sugar
1 egg, beaten lightly
⅔ cup (160ml) milk
20g butter, melted
2 tablespoons finely chopped
   fresh chives
4 thick gourmet sausages (500g)
40g butter, extra
2 large brown onions (400g),
   sliced thinly
2 tablespoons brown sugar
½ cup (140g) tomato relish
1 tablespoon coarsely chopped
   fresh chives, extra

1 Combine flour and sugar in small bowl; gradually whisk in egg and milk until mixture is smooth. Stir in butter and chives.
2 Drop teaspoons of batter into large heated non-stick frying pan; cook, in batches, until browned lightly both sides.
3 Reheat same cleaned frying pan; cook sausages until browned and cooked as desired. Slice each sausage into 12 pieces; cover to keep warm.
4 Heat extra butter in same cleaned frying pan; cook onion, stirring, about 10 minutes or until just browned. Add brown sugar; cook, stirring, about 5 minutes or until onion caramelises.
5 Top each pancake with ½ teaspoon relish, one slice of the sausage and a little caramelised onion. Sprinkle with extra chives.
6 Serve hot.

makes 48
per pancake 3.9g fat;
240kJ (57 cal)

ham and artichoke risotto cakes

PREPARATION TIME 20 MINUTES **COOKING TIME** 45 MINUTES

DO AHEAD Risotto can be spread on a tray and refrigerated a day ahead.

¾ cup (180ml) dry white wine
1½ cups (375ml) beef stock
2½ cups (625ml) water
20g butter
1 medium brown onion (150g),
    chopped finely
2 cloves garlic, crushed
2 cups (400g) arborio rice
1 cup (80g) finely grated
    parmesan cheese
2 cups (200g) packaged
    breadcrumbs
vegetable oil, for shallow-frying
1½ cups (390g) bottled
    tomato pasta sauce
1 teaspoon sambal oelek
150g shaved ham
250g bottled marinated
    artichokes, sliced thinly

1 Heat wine, stock and the water
   in large saucepan; cover.
2 Melt butter in large saucepan;
   cook onion and garlic until soft.
   Add rice and 1 cup hot stock
   mixture; stir, over low heat, until
   liquid is absorbed. Keep adding
   hot stock mixture, in batches,
   stirring until absorbed. It will
   take about 35 minutes until
   rice is tender. Stir in cheese.
3 Spread risotto onto tray; cool.
4 Shape tablespoons of risotto into
   cakes, coat with breadcrumbs.
5 Heat oil in large frying pan;
   shallow-fry cakes, in batches,
   until browned both sides,
   drain on absorbent paper.
6 Preheat oven to hot. Place
   cakes on oiled oven trays; divide
   combined sauce and sambal
   among cakes, top with ham and
   artichoke. Bake, uncovered, in
   hot oven 5 minutes. Serve hot.

makes 64
per cake 4.2g fat; 344kJ (82 cal)

goes well with
risotto-filled zucchini flowers (page 110)
bruschetta niçoise (page 28)

filet mignons with béarnaise sauce

PREPARATION TIME 40 MINUTES **COOKING TIME** 30 MINUTES

2 x 250g packets picnic slices bacon

1/3 cup (90g) pesto

700g piece beef eye fillet, trimmed, cut into 2.5cm cubes

BEARNAISE SAUCE

1/4 cup (60ml) white wine vinegar

8 black peppercorns

1 tablespoon finely chopped green onions

2 tablespoons water

2 tablespoons finely chopped fresh tarragon

3 egg yolks

200g unsalted butter, melted

DO AHEAD Uncooked fillet mignons can be assembled a day ahead. Cover; refrigerate until required.

You need 40 toothpicks with two-pointed ends for this recipe.

1 Cut bacon into 2cm x 14cm strips.

2 Spread a little pesto on one side of each bacon strip; wrap one strip, pesto-side against the beef, around each piece of beef, secure with a toothpick. Cook filet mignons, in batches, on heated oiled grill plate (or grill or barbecue) until browned both sides and cooked as desired.

3 Serve hot with béarnaise sauce.

BEARNAISE SAUCE Place vinegar, peppercorns, onion, the water and half of the tarragon in small saucepan; bring to a boil. Reduce heat; simmer, uncovered, until liquid is reduced to 2 tablespoons. Strain liquid into small jug; discard solids. Place egg yolks in small heatproof bowl over small saucepan of simmering water; do not allow water to touch base of bowl. Whisk in reserved liquid; add butter in a thin, steady stream, whisking constantly until mixture thickens slightly. Stir in remaining tarragon.

makes 40

per filet mignon 2.8g fat; 216kJ (52 cal)

per tablespoon sauce 7.5g fat; 290kJ (69 cal)

goes well with

mini prawn cocktails (page 32)

pea puree potato bites (page 82)

chile con queso

PREPARATION TIME 10 MINUTES **COOKING TIME** 10 MINUTES

Serve chile con queso with a bowl of crispy corn chips.

2 teaspoons vegetable oil
½ small green capsicum (75g), chopped finely
½ small brown onion (40g), chopped finely
1 tablespoon drained bottled jalapeño chillies, chopped finely
1 clove garlic, crushed
½ x 400g can undrained chopped peeled tomatoes
250g packet cream cheese, softened

1 Heat oil in medium saucepan; cook capsicum, onion, chilli and garlic, stirring, until onion softens. Add tomato; cook, stirring, 2 minutes.
2 Add cheese; whisk until cheese melts and dip is smooth.
3 Serve hot.

makes 2 cups
per tablespoon
3.9g fat; 174kJ (42 cal)

goes well with
artichoke and roasted capsicum bruschetta (page 29)
chorizo taquitos with chilli tomato salsa (page 71)

rumaki

PREPARATION TIME 20 MINUTES (PLUS REFRIGERATION TIME) **COOKING TIME** 10 MINUTES

DO AHEAD Chicken livers can be marinated a day ahead. Cover; refrigerate until required.

You need 40 toothpicks with two-pointed ends for this recipe.

300g chicken livers, trimmed
2 tablespoons light soy sauce
2 tablespoons dry sherry
2 tablespoons lemon juice
1 clove garlic, crushed
1 teaspoon grated fresh ginger
4 bacon rashers (280g)
¼ cup (50g) drained water
    chestnut slices

1 Cut livers into 2cm pieces; combine with soy sauce, sherry, juice, garlic and ginger in medium bowl. Cover; refrigerate 2 hours.
2 Heat large frying pan; cook liver mixture, stirring, about 5 minutes or until just tender. Drain livers, discard marinade; cool.
3 Slice each bacon rasher into eight strips. Wrap one bacon strip around one piece of liver and one slice water chestnut; secure with toothpick. Repeat with remaining bacon, liver and water chestnuts.
4 Cook rumaki under hot grill until bacon is crisp.
5 Serve hot.

makes 32
per rumaki 2.1g fat;
187kJ (45 cal)

goes well with
chicken teriyaki mini
maki (page 49)
gyoza with soy vinegar
sauce (page 86)

fish cakes with mirin dipping sauce

PREPARATION TIME 20 MINUTES (PLUS REFRIGERATION TIME) **COOKING TIME** 20 MINUTES

DO AHEAD Uncooked fishcakes can be prepared and dipping sauce made a day ahead. Cover; refrigerate until required.

We recommend using redfish or flathead fillets for this recipe.

1kg boneless skinless fish fillets
3 green onions, chopped finely
2 cloves garlic, crushed
¼ cup coarsely chopped
   fresh coriander
2 tablespoons red curry paste
1 egg
¼ cup (60ml) coconut milk
100g green beans, sliced thinly
peanut oil, for shallow-frying
²/₃ cup (160ml) mirin
⅓ cup (80ml) salt-reduced
   soy sauce
2 green onions, chopped
   finely, extra

1 Blend or process fish, onion, garlic, coriander, paste, egg and coconut milk until just combined. Stir beans into mixture.
2 Using hands, shape level tablespoons of fish mixture into cakes, place on tray, cover; refrigerate 30 minutes.
3 Heat oil in large frying pan; shallow-fry fish cakes, in batches, about 3 minutes or until lightly browned both sides and cooked through (do not overcook or fish cakes will become rubbery). Drain on absorbent paper.
4 Combine mirin, soy sauce and extra green onion in small serving bowl.
5 Serve hot with mirin sauce.

makes 56
per fish cake 2.8g fat;
174kJ (42 cal)
per tablespoon sauce
0g fat; 64kJ (15 cal)

goes well with
thai coconut prawns (page 61)
thai chicken salad in crispy
wonton cups (page 26)

scallops st jacques-style

PREPARATION TIME 5 MINUTES **COOKING TIME** 15 MINUTES

DO AHEAD Scallops can be cleaned up to 4 hours ahead. Cover; refrigerate until required. Buy or borrow 24 Chinese porcelain spoons for serving.

24 scallops (500g), roe removed
½ cup (125ml) dry white wine
½ cup (125ml) cream
1 tablespoon fresh
    chervil leaves

1 Rinse scallops under cold water. Dry scallops on absorbent paper.
2 Bring wine to a boil in medium frying pan; reduce heat then simmer until reduced by half. Whisk in cream; bring to a boil. Reduce heat; simmer, uncovered, about 5 minutes or until liquid has reduced by two-thirds. Add scallops; cook 1 minute. Remove from heat.
3 Place one scallop on each spoon; place on serving tray before spooning some of the sauce over each scallop. Top with chervil leaves.
4 Serve hot.

makes 24
per scallop 2.4g fat;
142kJ (34 cal)

goes well with
haloumi and tapenade
bruschetta (page 29)
grilled salmon on lemon
grass skewers (page 66)

risotto-filled zucchini flowers

PREPARATION TIME 50 MINUTES **COOKING TIME** 50 MINUTES

DO AHEAD Risotto can be prepared a day ahead.
Spread risotto on tray, cover; refrigerate until required

1 cup (250ml) dry white wine
2 cups (500ml) vegetable stock
1/2 cup (125ml) water
1 tablespoon olive oil
1 small brown onion (80g), chopped finely
1 clove garlic, crushed
1 cup (200g) arborio rice
150g mushrooms, sliced thinly
2 trimmed silverbeet leaves (160g), chopped finely
1/4 cup (20g) finely grated parmesan cheese
48 tiny zucchini with flowers attached
cooking-oil spray

1 Combine wine, stock and the water in large saucepan; bring to a boil.
Reduce heat; simmer, covered, to keep hot.
2 Meanwhile, heat oil in large saucepan; cook onion and garlic, stirring,
until onion softens. Add rice; stir to coat in onion mixture. Stir in 1 cup
of the hot stock mixture; cook, stirring, over low heat until liquid is
absorbed. Continue adding hot stock mixture, in 1-cup batches,
stirring, until liquid is absorbed after each addition. Total cooking
time should be about 35 minutes or until rice is tender.
3 Add mushrooms and silverbeet; cook, stirring, until mushrooms are
just tender. Stir in cheese.
4 Remove and discard stamens from centre of flowers; fill flowers with
risotto, twist petal tops to enclose filling.
5 Cook zucchini with flowers, in batches, on heated oiled grill plate
(or grill or barbecue) until zucchini are just tender and risotto is
heated through.
6 Serve hot.

makes 48
per flower 0.7g fat; 121kJ (29 cal)

goes well with
fried ravioli bolognese (page 74)
bocconcini, olive and cherry tomato skewers with pesto (page 34)

A flat, flaky, palm-shaped French pastry, palmiers were originally made as a sweet with caramelised sugar. Here are three of our savoury favourites.

palmiers

PREPARATION TIME
20 MINUTES (PLUS REFRIGERATION TIME)
COOKING TIME 15 MINUTES

DO AHEAD Palmiers can be assembled (but not cut), wrapped in plastic wrap and refrigerated for up to five hours before baking. Bring to room temperature and remove plastic before slicing and baking.

2 sheets ready-rolled puff pastry
1 portion of any of the 3 fillings, at right

1 Spread half of the filling on one sheet of pastry; fold two opposite sides of the pastry inward to meet in the middle, flatten slightly. Fold each side in half again to meet in the middle; press gently to flatten. Roll each side of folded pastry into the centre; flatten slightly. Repeat with remaining piece of pastry and filling. Enclose separately in plastic wrap; refrigerate on a tray for 1 hour.
2 Preheat oven to very hot. Lightly oil two oven trays.
3 Cut pastry rolls into 1.5cm slices. Place slices flat on prepared trays about 1.5cm apart. Bake, uncovered, in very hot oven about 12 minutes or until palmiers are browned lightly.
4 Serve hot.

bacon and sun-dried tomato

PREPARATION TIME 10 MINUTES
COOKING TIME 5 MINUTES

DO AHEAD Filling can be made a day ahead. Cover; refrigerate until required.

1 tablespoon olive oil
1 clove garlic, crushed
3 bacon rashers (210g), chopped finely
3 green onions, chopped finely
2 tablespoons sun-dried tomato pesto
2 tablespoons finely chopped fresh basil
1/3 cup (25g) finely grated parmesan cheese

1 Heat oil in medium frying pan; cook garlic and bacon, stirring, until bacon is crisp. Add onion and pesto; cook, stirring, 2 minutes.
2 Stir basil and cheese into bacon mixture; cool.

makes 32
per palmier 3.3g fat; 231kJ (55 cal)

mushroom and herb

PREPARATION TIME 10 MINUTES
COOKING TIME 10 MINUTES

DO AHEAD Filling can be made a day ahead.
Cover; refrigerate until required.

60g butter
2 teaspoons olive oil
250g button mushrooms, chopped finely
1 tablespoon plain flour
2 tablespoons finely chopped fresh chives
1 tablespoon finely chopped fresh tarragon
1/4 teaspoon freshly ground black pepper

1   Heat butter and oil in medium saucepan; cook
     mushrooms, stirring, until liquid evaporates.
     Add flour; cook, stirring, 2 minutes.
2   Stir in remaining ingredients; cool.

makes 32
per palmier 3.9g fat; 227kJ (54 cal)

cream cheese and green olive

PREPARATION TIME 10 MINUTES

DO AHEAD Filling can be made a day ahead.
Cover; refrigerate until required.

1/2 cup (75g) pimento-stuffed green olives
100g packaged cream cheese, softened
1 tablespoon lemon juice

1   Finely chop olives.
2   Combine olives in small bowl with cheese and juice.

makes 32
per palmier 3.3g fat; 199kJ (48 cal)

DO AHEAD Pizza base can be cut into rounds a day ahead: keep airtight at room temperature.
Pizzas can be assembled up to 2 hours before baking. Cover; refrigerate until required.

mascarpone and ham mini pizzas

PREPARATION TIME 20 MINUTES
COOKING TIME 10 MINUTES

335g (30cm) ready-made pizza base
2 tablespoons tomato paste
100g shaved leg ham
2 tablespoons mascarpone cheese
2 teaspoons finely chopped fresh chives

1 Preheat oven to moderately hot.
2 Using 4.5cm-round cutter, cut rounds from pizza base.
3 Place rounds on oven trays. Divide paste evenly over rounds; top with ham, cheese and chives. Bake, uncovered, in moderately hot oven about 5 minutes or until pizzas are heated through.
4 Serve hot.

makes 24
per pizza 1.7g fat; 302kJ (72 cal)

lamb and rocket mini pizzas

PREPARATION TIME 20 MINUTES
COOKING TIME 10 MINUTES

335g (30cm) ready-made pizza base
2 tablespoons tomato paste
70g firm goat cheese, sliced thinly
12 semi-dried tomatoes (85g), halved
140g cooked lamb fillet, sliced thinly
24 baby rocket leaves, sliced finely

1 Preheat oven to moderately hot.
2 Using 4.5cm-round cutter, cut rounds from pizza base.
3 Place rounds on oven trays. Divide paste evenly over rounds; top with cheese. Bake, uncovered, in moderately hot oven about 5 minutes or until pizzas are heated through. Top with tomato, lamb and rocket.
4 Serve hot.

makes 24
per pizza 1.9g fat; 359kJ (86 cal)

blue cheese and green onion mini pizzas

PREPARATION TIME 20 MINUTES
COOKING TIME 10 MINUTES

335g (30cm) ready-made pizza base
2 tablespoons tomato paste
2 green onions, sliced thinly
75g danish blue cheese, chopped coarsely

1   Preheat oven to moderately hot.
2   Using 4.5cm-round cutter, cut rounds from
    pizza base.
3   Place rounds on oven trays. Divide paste evenly
    over rounds; top with onion and cheese. Bake,
    uncovered, in moderately hot oven about
    5 minutes or until pizzas are heated through.
4   Serve hot.

makes 24
per pizza 1.8g fat; 302kJ (72 cal)

greek mini pizzas

PREPARATION TIME 20 MINUTES
COOKING TIME 10 MINUTES

335g (30cm) ready-made pizza base
2 tablespoons tomato paste
1/2 cup (80g) halved seeded kalamata olives
150g drained bottled char-grilled red capsicum
70g fetta cheese, crumbled
24 small basil leaves

1   Preheat oven to moderately hot.
2   Using 4.5cm-round cutter, cut rounds from
    pizza base.
3   Place rounds on oven trays. Divide paste evenly
    over rounds; top with olives, capsicum and cheese.
    Bake, uncovered, in moderately hot oven about
    5 minutes or until pizzas are heated through.
    Top with basil.
4   Serve hot.

makes 24
per pizza 1.7g fat; 312kJ (75 cal)

glossary

angostura bitters a popular brand of bitters; an aromatic essence of herbs, roots and bark used for flavouring cocktails, etc.

bacon

RASHERS also known as slices of bacon, made from smoked, cured pork side.

PICNIC SLICES vacuum-packed, smoked, cured shoulder bacon.

baileys a cream liqueur made with Irish whiskey.

baking powder a raising agent consisting mainly of two parts cream of tartar to one part bicarbonate of soda (baking soda).

beans

GREEN sometimes called french or string beans.

MEXICAN-STYLE a canned mixture of kidney, haricot or pinto beans cooked with tomato, peppers, onion, garlic and various spices.

REFRIED twice-cooked pinto beans: soaked and boiled then mashed and fried, traditionally in lard. Available canned in supermarkets.

bread

MINI TOASTS small, toasted bread slices. Available from supermarkets and delis.

NAAN leavened bread that is baked on the inside wall of a tandoor or clay oven.

PITTA also known as lebanese bread; wheat-flour pocket bread sold in large, flat pieces that separate into two thin rounds. Also available as pocket pitta.

PUMPERNICKEL slightly sour bread made with molasses, rye and wheat flours.

breadcrumbs

PACKAGED fine-textured, crunchy, purchased, white breadcrumbs.

STALE day-old bread made into crumbs by grating, blending or processing.

burghul also known as bulghur wheat; hulled steamed wheat kernels that are dried, then crushed.

butter use salted or unsalted ("sweet") butter; 125g is equal to one stick.

buttermilk originally the liquid left after cream was separated from milk; today, made similarly to yogurt.

cabanossi also known as cabana; sausage that is ready to eat.

capers grey-green buds of a shrub; sold dried and salted or pickled in brine.

capsicum also known as bell pepper or, simply, pepper. Discard seeds and membranes before use.

caraway seeds member of the parsley family; available in seed or ground form.

cayenne pepper a long, very hot red chilli; usually sold dried and ground.

cheese

BLUE mould-treated cheeses mottled with blue veining.

BOCCONCINI walnut-sized, baby mozzarella; delicate, semi-soft, white cheese. Spoils rapidly so keep in refrigerator, in brine, for one or two days at most.

BRIE has a bloomy white rind and a creamy centre.

CHEDDAR a common cow-milk "tasty" cheese; aged and hard with a "bite".

FARM varies in texture, can be mild and sliceable or dry and crumbly.

FETTA a crumbly goat- or sheep-milk cheese with a sharp, salty taste.

FONTINA a smooth firm cheese with a nutty taste and a brown or red rind.

GOAT made from goat milk, has an earthy, strong taste; available soft and firm.

GORGONZOLA cow-milk blue cheese; white to yellow in colour with bluish marbling.

GRUYERE a Swiss cheese with small holes and a nutty, slightly salty flavour.

HALOUMI a cream-coloured, firm, sheep-milk cheese matured in brine.

MASCARPONE a cultured cream product; whitish to creamy-yellow in colour.

MOZZARELLA a semi-soft cheese with a delicate, fresh taste.

NEUFCHATEL similar in flavour and appearance to cream cheese, but contains less fat and more moisture.

PACKAGED CREAM known as Philadelphia or Philly; a soft cow-milk cheese.

PARMESAN a sharp-tasting, dry, hard cheese, made from skim or part-skim milk; aged for at least a year.

RICOTTA a soft, white, cow-milk cheese; has sweet flavour and grainy texture

SWISS generic name for a variety of Swiss cheeses.

chervil also known as cicily; herb with mild fennel flavour and curly leaves.

chillies available in many varieties and sizes, both fresh and dried. Generally, the smaller the chilli, the hotter it is. Use rubber gloves when seeding and chopping fresh chillies as they can burn your skin.

FLAKES crushed, dried chillies.

JALAPENO sold chopped or whole, bottled in vinegar, as well as fresh.

POWDER made from ground chillies.

RED THAI small, medium-hot, bright-red chillies.

SAUCE our recipes use a hot Chinese variety made of chillies, salt and vinegar.

SWEET CHILLI SAUCE mild, sauce made from chillies, sugar, garlic and vinegar.

chinese cabbage also known as peking cabbage or wong bok.

chorizo sausage made of coarsely ground pork, garlic and chillies.

coconut

MILK pure, unsweetened coconut milk; available in cans and cartons.

MILK POWDER coconut milk that's been dehydrated and ground to a fine powder.

cointreau French liqueur; orange-flavoured brandy.

coriander also known as cilantro or Chinese parsley; leafy, green herb.

cornflour also known as cornstarch; used as a thickening agent.

cornichons French for "gherkin", cornichons are tiny pickled gherkins.

cranberry sauce, whole-berry bottled mix of water, cranberries and sucrose.

crème de cacao liqueur made from cocoa beans and vanilla.

curaçao orange liqueur; white (clear), orange, red, green and blue versions are available.

curry paste commercial pastes, from mild tikka and medium madras to fiery vindaloo. Use whichever suits your chilli tolerance.

RED contains red chilli, soy bean oil, onion, garlic, lemon rind, shrimp paste, paprika, cumin, turmeric and pepper.

TANDOORI contains garlic, tamarind, ginger, coriander, chilli and spices.

TIKKA contains chilli, cumin, coriander, lentil flour, garlic, ginger, oil, turmeric, fennel, pepper, cloves, cinnamon and cardamom.

curry powder commercial blend of ground spices.

egg some recipes call for raw or barely cooked eggs; if there is a salmonella in your area, use caution.

eggplant also known as aubergine.

fennel also known as anise or finocchio; vegetable eaten raw in salads or braised or fried as an accompaniment.

fish sauce also called nam pla or nuoc nam; made from pulverised, salted, fermented fish, most often anchovies.

flour

BUCKWHEAT although not a true cereal, flour is made from its seeds. Available from health food stores.

PLAIN an all-purpose flour, made from wheat.

SELF-RAISING plain flour sifted with baking powder in proportion of 1 cup flour to 2 tsp baking powder.

framboise liqueur raspberry-flavoured liqueur.

ginger also known as root or green ginger.

gow gee pastry wonton wrappers. Substitute spring roll or egg pastry sheets.

grand marnier orange-flavoured liqueur.

hoisin sauce thick, sweet Chinese paste.

horseradish, prepared grated horseradish with flavourings; do not confuse with horseradish cream.

ice magic a fast-setting chocolate coating.

kahlua a brandy-based, coffee-flavoured liqueur.

kalamata olives small brine-cured black olives.

kecap manis also known as ketjap manis; Indonesian thick soy sauce.

kumara Polynesian name of orange sweet potato.

lamington pan 20cm x 30cm slab cake pan, 3cm deep.

lemon grass lemon-tasting grass; use the white lower part of each stem.

mince meat also known as ground meat.

mirin sweet rice wine used in Japanese cooking; not to be confused with sake.

mushrooms

FLAT large, flat mushrooms with a rich earthy flavour.

SHIITAKE also sold as donko mushrooms; available fresh and dried.

mustard

DIJON a pale brown, distinctively flavoured, fairly mild French mustard.

WHOLEGRAIN also known as seeded. A coarse-grain mustard made from crushed mustard seeds and dijon-style French mustard.

oil

OLIVE made from ripened olives. Extra virgin and virgin are the best, while extra light or light refers to the taste of the product, not the amount of fat.

PEANUT pressed from ground peanuts; has high smoke point.

SESAME made from roasted white sesame seeds; used as a flavouring only.

oyster sauce made from oysters and their brine, salt, soy sauce and starches.

palm sugar also known as jaggery, gula jawa and gula melaka; ranges from white to dark-brown in colour. Usually sold in rock-hard cakes. Substitute dark brown sugar, if necessary.

pancetta Italian bacon that is cured, but not smoked.

paprika ground dried red capsicum (bell pepper), available sweet or hot.

pastry

FILLO also known as phyllo; tissue-thin pastry sheets purchased chilled or frozen.

PUFF (READY-ROLLED) packaged sheets of frozen puff pastry.

SHORTCRUST (READY-ROLLED) packaged sheets of frozen shortcrust pastry.

TARTLETS miniature cases made of shortcrust pastry.

pine nuts also known as pignoli; small kernels from cones of some pine trees.

polenta cereal made of ground corn (maize); also the name of dish made from it.

potato, tiny new also known as chats. Harvested young; have thin, waxy, skin.

prawn also known as shrimp.

prosciutto cured, air-dried (unsmoked), pressed ham.

radicchio burgundy-leaved lettuce with white ribs and slightly bitter flavour.

red pepper mix also known as shichimi togarashi or seven-spice mix; based on hot peppers, black hemp or white poppy seeds, sansho pepper, mandarin peel, nori and white sesame seeds.

rice

ARBORIO small, round-grain rice well suited to absorb a large amount of liquid.

KOSHIHIKARI small, round-grain white rice.

rice paper sheets an edible, translucent paper made from water and the pith of the rice-paper plant.

rocket also known as arugula, rugula and rucola; peppery green leaf. Baby rocket is also available.

roe fish eggs.

rum distillation of fermented sugar cane.

sake rice wine used in cooking or as a drink. If unavailable, substitute dry sherry, vermouth or brandy.

sambal oelek (also ulek or olek) salty chilli paste; Indonesian in origin.

sashimi skinless, boneless raw fish pieces.

sauerkraut fermented mix of shredded cabbage, salt and spices; available ready-made in supermarkets.

seafood the seafood in some sushi recipes in this book has not been cooked.

seaweed, toasted also known as yaki-nori; available already toasted. Can be frozen, refrigerated or stored in an airtight container.

sesame seeds tiny oval seeds available in black and white variations.

sherry, dry fortified wine.

silverbeet also known as Swiss chard or chard; leafy, dark-green vegetable with thick white stems and ribs.

snow peas also known as mange tout ("eat all").

spinach also known as english spinach and, incorrectly, silverbeet. Baby spinach leaves are also available.

spring roll wrappers also known as egg roll wrappers. Purchase fresh or frozen from Asian supermarkets

soy sauce made from fermented soy beans.

JAPANESE less dense and salty than Chinese soy.

sugar

BROWN finely granulated sugar retaining molasses for its characteristic colour.

CASTER also known as superfine or finely granulated table sugar.

sumac a purple-red spice with a tart, lemony flavour.

tabasco brand name of an extremely fiery sauce made from hot red peppers.

tamarind paste sour, ready-to-use paste from the pulp of the tamarind bean.

tapenade a thick paste made from olives, olive oil, lemon, capers and spices.

teriyaki sauce made from soy sauce, mirin, sugar, ginger and other spices.

tequila made from distilled agave juice (pulque).

tomato

CHERRY also known as Tiny Tim or Tom Thumb tomato.

EGG also called plum or roma; small and oval.

GRAPE small, grape-shaped tomatoes.

PASTE triple-concentrated tomato puree.

SAUCE also known as ketchup or catsup.

SEMI-DRIED partially dried tomatoes, in olive oil.

tortilla thin unleavened bread rounds; available as corn tortillas or flour tortillas.

vermouth a herb-flavoured fortified white wine.

vinegar

BALSAMIC from Modena, Italy; made from wine of Trebbiano grapes and aged to give a pungent flavour.

CHINESE RED an Asian salty vinegar.

RED WINE based on fermented red wine.

RICE made from fermented rice; colourless and flavoured with sugar, salt. Also known as seasoned rice vinegar.

WHITE WINE made from white wine.

vodka clear spirit distilled from grains.

wasabi Asian horseradish sold as a powder or paste.

water chestnuts small brown tubers with a crisp, white, nutty-tasting flesh.

wonton wrappers substitute gow gee, egg or spring roll wrappers.

worcestershire sauce thin, dark-brown spicy sauce.

yogurt we used unflavoured full-fat yogurt in our recipes.

zucchini also known as courgette, belonging to the squash family. Zucchini flowers are also available.

index

facts and figures

Wherever you live, you'll be able to use our recipes with the help of these easy-to-follow conversions. While these conversions are approximate only, the difference between an exact and the approximate conversion of various liquid and dry measures is minimal and will not affect your cooking results.

dry measures

metric	imperial
15g	1/2oz
30g	1oz
60g	2oz
90g	3oz
125g	4oz (1/4lb)
155g	5oz
185g	6oz
220g	7oz
250g	8oz (1/2lb)
280g	9oz
315g	10oz
345g	11oz
375g	12oz (3/4lb)
410g	13oz
440g	14oz
470g	15oz
500g	16oz (1lb)
750g	24oz (11/2lb)
1kg	32oz (2lb)

oven temperatures

These oven temperatures are only a guide. Always check the manufacturer's manual.

	°C (Celsius)	°F (Fahrenheit)	Gas Mark
Very slow	120	250	1
Slow	150	300	2
Moderately slow	160	325	3
Moderate	180 - 190	350 - 375	4
Moderately hot	200 - 210	400 - 425	5
Hot	220 - 230	450 - 475	6
Very hot	240 - 250	500 - 525	7

liquid measures

metric	imperial
30ml	1 fluid oz
60ml	2 fluid oz
100ml	3 fluid oz
125ml	4 fluid oz
150ml	5 fluid oz (1/4 pint/1 gill)
190ml	6 fluid oz
250ml	8 fluid oz
300ml	10 fluid oz (1/2 pint)
500ml	16 fluid oz
600ml	20 fluid oz (1 pint)
1000ml (1 litre)	13/4 pints

helpful measures

metric	imperial
3mm	1/8in
6mm	1/4in
1cm	1/2in
2cm	3/4in
2.5cm	1in
5cm	2in
6cm	21/2in
8cm	3in
10cm	4in
13cm	5in
15cm	6in
18cm	7in
20cm	8in
23cm	9in
25cm	10in
28cm	11in
30cm	12in (1ft)

measuring equipment

The difference between one country's measuring cups and another's is, at most, within a 2 or 3 teaspoon variance. (For the record, 1 Australian metric measuring cup holds approximately 250ml.) The most accurate way of measuring dry ingredients is to weigh them. When measuring liquids, use a clear glass or plastic jug with the metric markings. (One Australian metric tablespoon holds 20ml; one Australian metric teaspoon holds 5ml.)

If you would like to purchase *The Australian Women's Weekly* Test Kitchen's metric measuring cups and spoons (as approved by Standards Australia), turn to page 120 for details and order coupon. You will receive:
- a graduated set of four cups for measuring dry ingredients, with sizes marked on the cups.
- a graduated set of four spoons for measuring dry and liquid ingredients, with amounts marked on the spoons.

Note: North America, NZ and the UK use 15ml tablespoons. All cup and spoon measurements are level.

We use large eggs having an average weight of 60g.

how to measure

When using graduated metric measuring cups, shake dry ingredients loosely into the appropriate cup. Do not tap the cup on a bench or tightly pack the ingredients unless directed to do so. Level top of measuring cups and measuring spoons with a knife. When measuring liquids, place a clear glass or plastic jug with metric markings on a flat surface to check accuracy at eye level.

Looking after **your interest...**

Keep your ACP cookbooks clean, tidy and within easy reach with slipcovers designed to hold up to 12 books. Plus you can follow our recipes perfectly with a set of accurate measuring cups and spoons, as used by *The Australian Women's Weekly* Test Kitchen.

To order

Mail or fax Photocopy and complete the coupon below and post to ACP Books Reader Offer, ACP Publishing, GPO Box 4967, Sydney NSW 2001, or fax to (02) 9267 4967.

Phone Have your credit card details ready, then phone 136 116 (Mon-Fri, 8.00am-6.00pm; Sat, 8.00am-6.00pm).

Price

Book Holder

Australia: $13.10 (incl. GST).
Elsewhere: $A21.95.

Metric Measuring Set

Australia: $6.50 (incl. GST).
New Zealand: $A8.00.
Elsewhere: $A9.95.

Prices include postage and handling.
This offer is available in all countries.

Payment

Australian residents

We accept the credit cards listed on the coupon, money orders and cheques.

Overseas residents

We accept the credit cards listed on the coupon, drafts in $A drawn on an Australian bank, and also British, New Zealand and U.S. cheques in the currency of the country of issue. Credit card charges are at the exchange rate current at the time of payment.

Test Kitchen Staff
Food director *Pamela Clark*
Food editor *Karen Hammial*
Assistant food editor *Amira Ibram*
Test kitchen managers *Kimberley Coverdale, Elizabeth Hooper*
Senior home economist *Kellie Ann*
Home economists *Kelly Cruickshanks, Vishnu Gaunder, Cathie Lonnie, Naomi Scesny, Jeanette Seamons, Alison Webb, Danielle West*
Editorial coordinator *Amanda Josling*

ACP Books Staff

Editorial director *Susan Tomnay*
Creative director *Hieu Chi Nguyen*
Senior editors *Linda Wilton, Julie Collard*
Designers *Mary Keep, Caryl Wiggins, Alison Windmill*
Studio manager *Caryl Wiggins*
Editorial/Sales coordinator *Caroline Lowry*
Editorial assistant *Karen Lai*
Publishing manager (sales) *Brian Cearnes*
Publishing manager (rights & new projects) *Jane Hazell*
Brand manager *Donna Gianniotis*
Pre-press *Harry Palmer*
Production manager *Carol Currie*
Business manager *Sally Lees*
Assistant business analyst *Martin Howes*
Chief executive officer *John Alexander*
Group publisher *Jill Baker*
Publisher *Sue Wannan*

Produced by ACP Books, Sydney.
Printed by Dai Nippon Printing in Korea.
Published by ACP Publishing Pty Limited, 54 Park St, Sydney; GPO Box 4088, Sydney, NSW 2001.
Ph: (02) 9282 8618 Fax: (02) 9267 9438.
acpbooks@acp.com.au
www.acpbooks.com.au
To order books, phone 136 116.
Send recipe enquiries to recipeenquiries@acp.com.au
AUSTRALIA: Distributed by Network Services, GPO Box 4088, Sydney, NSW 2001.
Ph: (02) 9282 8777 Fax: (02) 9264 3278.
UNITED KINGDOM: Distributed by Australian Consolidated Press (UK), Moulton Park Business Centre, Red House Rd, Moulton Park, Northampton, NN3 6AQ
Ph: (01604) 497 531 Fax: (01604) 497 533
acpukltd@aol.com
CANADA: Distributed by Whitecap Books Ltd, 351 Lynn Ave, North Vancouver, BC, V7J 2C4, Ph: (604) 980 9852.
NEW ZEALAND: Distributed by Netlink Distribution Company, Level 4, 23 Hargreaves St, College Hill, Auckland 1, Ph: (9) 302 7616.

Clark, Pamela.
New finger food.

Includes index.
ISBN 1 86396 282 4

1. Appetisers. I. Title.
II. Title: Australian Women's Weekly.

641.812

© ACP Publishing Pty Limited 2002
ABN 18 053 273 546
This publication is copyright. No part of it may be reproduced or transmitted in any form without the written permission of the publishers.
First published 2002. Reprinted 2003.

Photocopy and complete coupon below

☐ **Book Holder**

☐ **Metric Measuring Set**
   Please indicate number(s) required.

Mr/Mrs/Ms _____

Address _____

_____

Postcode _____ Country _____

Ph: Business hours ( ) _____

I enclose my cheque/money order for $ _____
payable to ACP Publishing.

OR: please charge my

☐ Bankcard   ☐ Visa   ☐ Mastercard

☐ Diners Club   ☐ American Express

Card number

Expiry date ____ /____

Cardholder's signature _____

Please allow up to 30 days delivery within Australia.
Allow up to 6 weeks for overseas deliveries.
Both offers expire 31/12/04. HLNFF03